Learning to Learn in a Second Language

Learning to Learn in a Second Language

Pauline Gibbons

HEINEMANN
Portsmouth, NH

PRIMARY ENGLISH TEACHING ASSOCIATION
NSW, Australia

Heinemann
A division of Reed Elsevier Inc.
361 Hanover Street
Portsmouth, NH 03801-3912
Offices and agents throughout the world

©1991 Primary English Teaching Association
Laura St, Newtown NSW 2042 Australia

First U.S. Printing 1993
ISBN 0-435-08785-1 (Heinemann)

Library of Congress Cataloging-in-Publication Data

Learning to learn in a second language / Pauline Gibbons.
    p. cm.
    Includes bibliographical references.
    ISBN 0-435-08785-1 (acid free paper)
    1. English language—Study and teaching—Foreign speakers.
2. Languages, Modern—Study and teaching.   3. Language in education.
4. Education, Bilingual.   I. Title.
PE1128.A2G47 1993
428'.007—dc20   92-40291
                                                            CIP

Cover design by Judi Pownall
Photographs by Christopher Simkin
Designed by Ken Shearman and Jeremy Steele
Edited by Jeremy Steele
Typeset in Galliard 11/13 by Bookserve Pty Ltd
1/637 Darling Street Rozelle NSW 2039

Printed in the United States of America on Acid Free Paper
04   03   02   VP   11   12   13

Contents

Acknowledgements

Many people have helped me in the writing of this book, and to all of them I would like to express my gratitude. They include colleagues, friends and writers, and those whose names do not appear in the bibliography but whose work has influenced my thinking about ESL education.

There are a number of people whom I would especially like to thank.

There have been many teachers who have shared their ideas, enthusiasm and expertise with me, and who have put many of the ideas in this book into practice in their classrooms. I am indebted to them, and to the children they teach. In particular I would like to thank St Mel's School, Campsie, who also assisted in providing the photographs.

Several friends offered valuable comments on the manuscript, and I thank in particular Bill White, Val Delaney, Peggy Crocker and Jenny Fitzpatrick for their comments.

Viv Nicoll gave a great deal of encouragement and advice, especially in the early stages of writing when it was most needed, and I thank her and members of the PETA board for their suggestions.

I am especially grateful to Jeremy Steele, who has been a patient, rigorous and courteous editor and whose constructive advice has undoubtedly improved this book.

And finally I would like to thank my family — my sons Mark and Ben for their patience during many evenings and weekends of work, and my husband John, who gave advice and great support throughout the writing of the book.

Pauline Gibbons

CHAPTER ONE

Bilingual Children and the Language of the School

One in four of all children in Australian schools speak English as their second language. In many urban areas the figure is very much higher than this, and in some schools as many as ninety per cent of the students speak or are in contact with a language (or languages) other than English at home. Throughout this book such children will be referred to as *second language learners*, because they speak English as a second language, and also as *bilingual children*.

In everyday speech, the term 'bilingual' usually refers to fluency in two languages. However, it is used here to refer to the ability to communicate in two or more languages, and does not necessarily imply competence or fluency. Rather it reflects the reality that second language learners are operating in two language domains. The use of 'bilingual' is also intended to focus the reader's attention on the potential language skills of these children, and to avoid a label which may suggest deficit (such as *non*-English speaking background).

Children for whom English is a second language form a diverse group. They come from a wide variety of language and socioeconomic backgrounds and have varying degrees of competence in their mother tongue, ranging from the ability to understand it in familiar situations, but not to speak it, to full fluency and literacy. Students from any of the following categories can be included amongst the group of learners who are the subject of this book.

Students newly arrived in Australia who come from a language background other than English.

These students may have had a variety of experiences. They may, for example:

- have spent time in a refugee camp
- have had periods of interrupted schooling
- have had no previous schooling
- have developed good oracy and literacy skills in their first language
- have had some experience with written English but lack oral skills.

Students born in Australia who enter school with little or no English.

Many kindergarten children can be included in this category.

Students who have had all or some of their schooling in Australia, and whose home background includes at least one language other than English.

Children in this group, who may have been born in Australia or elsewhere, come from homes where:

- English is not used
- English is not the only language used
- English is used as a second language between parents who do not speak the same first language.

Many of them will have developed some skills in spoken and written English, and may be very fluent in the language of the playground. However, their skills may not yet be adequate to cope fully with the language demands of the curriculum. There will also be others within this group who enter school with a good command of both English and their first language.

Being bilingual — an advantage or a disadvantage?

There is some evidence to suggest that competent bilinguals — those with good skills in two languages — have several advantages over monolinguals. Having two well-developed languages appears to result in a greater capacity for lateral thinking and problem solving, and bilinguals also seem to have greater facility in learning additional languages. The McGill University psychologists Lambert and Peal (1962) have suggested that where there is good literacy development in both languages, bilinguals on average score higher than monolinguals in verbal and non-verbal tests of intelligence. Having a second language also means having access to another world of people, ideas, ways of thinking and literature. Being a competent bilingual is a bonus, or as one teacher commented, bilinguals can think and say twice as much!

But most bilingual children, with the exception of those learning in a bilingual program, are at a disadvantage in school because they are expected to learn in their second (and on entry to school, usually their weaker) language. At age five, or whenever they enter school, and after they have come a long way in mastering their first language, they have suddenly to begin to learn a new language — English. Not only must they learn this new language, but they must learn *in* it as well. And they must immediately begin to use it to develop new and sometimes quite abstract concepts as well as literacy skills. Hence the title of this book, *Learning to Learn in a Second Language.*

It has often been assumed that children, particularly very young children, will simply 'pick up' a second language. Many teachers comment on how quickly children with limited or no English learn to communicate with their peers in the playground, and it is true that informal learning environments have a very influential role in the development of proficiency in English — particularly the everyday language that is essential for basic communication. So in the playground situation a newly arrived child often becomes quite fluent surprisingly quickly, and may soon be indistinguishable from his or her peers. This playground language includes the language which enables children to make friends, join in games and take part in a variety of day-to-day activities that develop and maintain social contacts. It usually occurs in face-to-face contact, and is thus highly dependent on the physical and visual context, and on gesture and body language. Fluency with this kind of language is an important part of language development; without it a child is isolated from the normal social life of the playground. Because the language tends to occur in situations in which meaning is made clear through the visual context, and because there is usually a strong motivation for the learner to learn, children tend to develop it quickly and seemingly quite effortlessly, and certainly without deliberate and planned teaching.

But playground language is very different from the language that teachers use in the classroom, and from the language that we expect children to learn to use. The language of the playground is not the language associated with learning in mathematics, or social studies, or science. The playground situation does not normally offer children the opportunity to use such language as: *if we increase the angle by 5 degrees, we could cut the circumference into equal parts.* Nor does it normally require the language associated with the higher order thinking skills, such as hypothesising, evaluating, inferring, generalising, predicting or classifying. Yet these are the language functions which are related to learning and the development of cognition; they occur in all areas of the curriculum, and without them a child's potential in academic areas cannot be realised.

Unlike the language of the playground, the language associated with school learning takes a long time to develop: it is frequently quite abstract, and there may be fewer concrete visual clues to support meaning. So it may be as much as five years before children who enter school without English develop English skills which are comparable to those of their peers. Learning a language is a long process, and unless the development of English is supported in all areas of the curriculum, these children will continue to be disadvantaged throughout their schooling, and beyond.

Who are the second language learners in my class?

Often children's fluency in the playground masks their real difficulties in English, and because they *sound* fluent in informal situations, their real language needs may go undetected. Many children become very good at hiding their difficulties and develop strategies that make them appear competent language users. They may use formulaic expressions or avoidance strategies in speaking, simply ignoring any communication that they do not understand. Often it is not until literacy and learning demands become greater, around Years 2 and 3, that language difficulties are first noticed, and then they may be seen as related to ability or behaviour. Recognising that a child's learning and literacy difficulties are *language-related* is an important first step in providing the necessary intervention and support and an appropriate class program.

Below is a list of some general characteristics associated with the English of some bilingual children. If you reflect on your own class, you may find that a number of children have difficulties similar to those listed here. Of course there will be some, including native speakers, who have genuine learning difficulties and whose language has similar features. However, it is likely that children whose language exhibits a large number of these characteristics are bilingual children whose English language skills are not yet adequate for the learning demands of the classroom. (It is of course important to recognise that it is possible to do something about this, and that such children are potentially as able to learn as the most competent English speakers in your class!)

Listening

- has difficulty following a series of instructions
- has a short concentration span, especially if the topic is unfamiliar
- appears to have difficulty predicting what is about to be said
- does not understand key words which alter meaning, such as *although, however, except, unless,* etc.
- has trouble distinguishing certain sounds.

Speaking

- has quite good oral language, and has mastered slang and playground language
- finds it difficult to adjust register, and may sound impolite in formal situations with adults
- uses language that is 'known' and therefore often says the same thing — for example, in 'newstime'
- makes mistakes with basic sentence structures — for example, *you told me where is it*

- makes grammatical mistakes not typical of an English speaker, such as mistakes in tense or with prepositions
- appears to have difficulty sequencing thoughts.

Reading

- reads slowly
- has poor comprehension if the topic is unfamiliar
- has trouble paraphrasing and isolating the main idea
- has difficulty reading for meaning, drawing conclusions and, in a narrative, predicting what will happen next
- rarely self-corrects when reading aloud.

Writing

- has generally poor written language skills, especially in subject areas
- can write sentences but has difficulty writing a paragraph or sequencing paragraphs
- writes only in an informal, 'chatty' style
- uses a limited vocabulary which lacks descriptive words
- uses simple sentence structures only
- makes grammatical errors not typical of a native speaker — for example, in word order, word endings, tense or prepositions
- spelling is poor
- lacks the confidence to write at length
- tends always to write the same thing (such as a simple recount) in free choice writing.

A distinction between what we have been calling playground and classroom language was first made by Skutnabb-Kangas and Toukamaa (1976) in a description of the academic performance of Finnish immigrant children living in Sweden. Their research is very relevant to the Australian situation, for the experience of these children parallels in many ways the experience of migrant children in Australia. The Finnish children had either been born in Sweden but spoke Finnish at home, or had immigrated at pre-school age (prior to age seven). Skutnabb-Kangas noted that many of these children had surface fluency in Swedish, which was their second language, and in everyday situations they could converse in age-appropriate ways in both their first and second languages. However, their skills in more academic language, and particularly in literacy, were much below age-appropriate levels in both languages. As Chapter 3 of this book suggests, it may be more useful to think of these two areas of language as being on a continuum rather than as being discrete, but the distinction between playground and classroom language is nevertheless an important one in relation to the English language development of bilingual children.

What is the role of the mother tongue in learning a second language?

If you have had older newly arrived children in your class, you may have noticed that many of them develop English surprisingly rapidly, not only learning to communicate in the playground, but also acquiring the more abstract language of the classroom. It seems clear that high levels of skill in the mother tongue, particularly when these include literacy, greatly facilitate the learning of English.

To bring this point home, think of a language that is quite unknown to you. Now imagine that someone is trying to teach you to tell the time in the new language. Because you are able to tell the time in English, and have already developed a range of concepts related to time and clocks and numbers, you would, while you are listening to your new language, be making connections with what you already know. Though the language itself is new to you, the concepts are familiar ones, and what you are developing in this situation is a new 'label' for old learning. Now imagine how much more difficult it would be to learn to tell the time in an unknown language if you had not first learned to do it in English, and perhaps had never seen a clock. Now there is nothing to peg your new language to, and it will be much harder for you to learn.

So, if you have sorted out the world in one language, it becomes much easier to sort it out again in a second language. Children who arrive in school with a strong command of their first language and a developed range of concepts in that language are thus in a very favourable position to learn English. They are adding on a second language to the one they already have (in much of the literature in the area they are referred to as 'additive bilinguals'). Younger children, whose language skills are less well developed, are in a less favourable position to learn a second language. With less conceptual and linguistic development, they have fewer pegs on which to hang new learning. It would seem that one of the worst times to switch language environments is around the age of five or six, when the comparative fragility of the first language does not support the learning of a second.

It should be made clear at this point that there is no inherent reason why very young children cannot develop two or more languages at the same time. Most people know children who happily use more than one language quite competently and have no difficulty in doing so. The key factor seems to be the degree to which the first language is continuing to develop. Where there is no threat to the first language, there appears to be no reason why other languages cannot also be learned at the same time to a high degree of competence.

However, the situation for many bilingual children who have little mother tongue support is that once they start school their mother tongue is gradually

Cross-grade tutoring benefits both children. Here Shirley (Year 5) is working with Margaret (Kindergarten).

replaced by English. Instead of adding on a language, they lose one. If their English is also not well developed, they can fall between two languages, with neither the first nor the second adequate for learning in school. Such children are clearly at risk, and perhaps most vulnerable are those who enter school in kindergarten with minimal English. For these children it is important that schools not only support the development of English, but also do all they can to provide support for the mother tongue. Chapter 6 offers some suggestions as to how this might be done.

Expect a lot!

One more key point must be made in this chapter: namely, that even when their language puts children at a potential disadvantage at school, they continue to have the same capacity for learning as all other children. Given appropriate school experiences and intervention, and high expectations by their teachers, they can and do achieve at the same levels as their peers who are already familiar with the language of the school. All children must develop the language associated with learning, and for bilingual children this must be a major focus. In practice it requires a classroom program with specific English language objectives in all areas of the curriculum, and a classroom environment which supports the acquisition of a second language.

However, many teachers may feel that their previous training and experience have not sufficiently prepared them for teaching in a multilingual classroom. Particularly in schools where there is no ESL specialist to consult, some teachers find their first encounter with children who speak little or no English a frustrating experience, and worry that they may not be giving them adequate support. If you are one of these teachers, you can feel reassured by the fact that learning a second language is in many ways similar to learning a first language, and that many of the principles and strategies are the same. If your classroom is supportive and caring, one where children feel comfortable and willing to participate, you already have a good language learning environment. The following chapters will offer some further suggestions about how the particular needs of children learning in their second language can be met within this environment.

CHAPTER TWO

Planning for a Language for Learning

Learning a second language

The question is often asked — is learning a second language the same as learning the first language? Most research would indicate the answer — yes and no.

How are the processes similar?

In many ways the acquisition of a second language parallels very closely the acquisition of a first. In both situations learners typically begin by using 'telegraphic' speech, relying mainly on 'content' words. They will say something like *want go play*, and at a later stage add the grammatical or 'function' words *I want to go out to play*.

In both first and second language learning there is a gradual approximation to standard forms of grammar. Learners appear to develop hypotheses about the language, which they later confirm or reject. Children in both situations might say, for example, *I goed* or *I runned*, having developed a hypothesis about the past tense ending (*I opened*, therefore *I goed*).

Many learners of both first and second languages rely heavily in the very early stages on chunks of language and routine phrases, gradually substituting new words or phrases as they are acquired. The toddler who says *all-gone-milk* has probably learned this as a single unit to express a single meaning in one situation. But once it is perceived as two separate units (*all-gone* and *milk*) the child is able to produce many variations: *all-gone ice cream*, *all-gone daddy* and so on. This process can also be observed in second language learners, and many early attempts rely on a memorised routine chunk of language, which is later separated out and expanded.

How are the processes different?

The significant differences between the two processes lie in the conditions under which they are commonly learned.

When a child is learning his or her first language, there are normally many opportunities to engage in one-to-one interaction with an adult. Almost all adults intuitively respond to the child by adjusting their own speech appropriately, and an adult who knows the child is very skilled at fine-tuning responses. These responses are tailored to the child's needs, and the child's approximations are accepted and interpreted. It is nearly impossible to duplicate the quality, quantity and density of these interactions in the classroom setting, where the teacher may be the only adult model, and where there are competing demands from other children.

In addition, children learning a second language at school are at a very different cognitive and conceptual level. By the time they start, they will have had wide experience of using language, not as an end in itself, but as a means of finding out about the world around them. They begin to learn their second language on the basis of this language experience, and so their learning in the early stages involves working out how to express familiar concepts and meanings in the new language.

There may also be a difference in terms of the psychological climate. The home is in general supportive of language learning, and children learning their first language 'risk-take' in a stress-free environment. By comparison the classroom may be stressful or threatening, and this may inhibit language learning as well as affecting self-esteem. Classroom anxiety is a very strong factor working against language learning.

Another major difference is the time-frame within which the second language must be learned. English-speaking children begin their school-learning in a familiar language which they have been hearing and using for around five years. They have had time and opportunity to use English constantly with a wide range of people and for a wide range of purposes. Second language learners have also been acquiring language and advancing cognitively — but not in English. In an English-only school they must make up this gap as quickly as possible if they are not to be disadvantaged.

Features of a supportive classroom

What characterises a classroom which is supportive of the second language learner? A number of principles can be inferred from this brief discussion of second language acquisition, and they are set out opposite. Not surprisingly, a classroom which is characterised by these features would support any child's language learning, but for bilingual children the type of classroom they describe is of special relevance.

The classroom provides a comfortable learning environment.

Learners' attitudes to learning and their confidence in themselves as learners are key factors in successful learning. Feeling confident to 'have a go', without fear of failure, and developing a positive attitude to learning itself allows learners to develop confidence in their abilities to learn, and the importance of this cannot be over-emphasised. Many bilingual children suffer low self-esteem because of early frustrations and language-related difficulties in school. A cycle of failure, low self-esteem and subsequent expectations of continued failure must not be allowed to develop. In addition, positive responses by teachers to children's first language and culture are important in enhancing learners' self-esteem and developing their confidence.

Language is used in the service of other learning, with planned integration of content and language.

In the same way as children learn a first language as a means of finding out about the world around them, rather than as an end in itself, so learning a second language seems to be most effective when the focus is on using language to learn about something else. There is a place for explicit discussion *about* language, but this is likely to be useful only in so far as it is related to the actual language being used by the learner.

There are planned opportunities for meaningful interaction between peers.

The peer group is a powerful resource to the learner, providing a wide range of models of language use, and the need to communicate offers the learner a real motivation to use language.

Children have opportunities to be 'problem solvers' rather than 'information receivers'.

This will involve collaborative learning, where the children are given responsibility for some of their own or the group's learning.

The models of language presented are understandable to the learner but also provide new ways of expressing meaning.

Learners must be able to hear models which will extend their own language use.

There are frequent opportunities for interaction between teacher and individual student.

In classrooms where there are large numbers of bilingual children and few good English models, the quality and quantity of personal interactions with the teacher becomes a major resource for children's language development.

The primary curriculum: a tool for language development

In the areas of the curriculum not traditionally thought of as language, such as maths, social studies, craft or science, the focus of planning and programming is often on the subject content. The themes, the knowledge and the 'facts' are what determine the resources we use and the activities we plan. Of course language is integral to most of what happens in the classroom, but to a competent language user its role is like that of a window, through which we look at the content. It is transparent, and although we may recognise that it is there, its transparency means that it is very hard to see. Focusing on content alone makes language the invisible curriculum in the school. And for children with poor English skills the language becomes a block to learning. To put it another way, their window is made of frosted glass. So, for children learning in a second language, it is important that we are aware of the language we use and that we deliberately create opportunities for children to hear and use it. We need to look at language rather than simply through it. The rest of this chapter will consider how to select and focus on language in all curriculum areas with the aim of developing the language that children will need for learning.

Language has always been regarded as an important focus for teaching, but often it has been removed from the broader learning context. Specific language areas have been taught in isolation from the rest of the curriculum, and often in isolation from each other as well. Spelling, dictation, comprehension, grammar and reading have at times been regarded as separate parts of the language program, unrelated to other areas of the curriculum such as science or mathematics.

The teaching of English as a second language has followed a similar pattern. Separate and isolated 'structural progressive' courses have been based on the idea that grammatical structures should be introduced in a hierarchical sequence, with those considered simple preceding those thought of as more difficult. In such courses the language itself is a separate subject within the curriculum. Often this has led to a mismatch between the language the children are expected to learn in the course and the actual language they need to participate in the classroom. For example, many structurally based courses introduce the present continuous verb form very early. (This is the *-ing* form of the verb, as in *I am running, jumping,* etc.) Its early position probably has more to do with the fact that it is easy to demonstrate and teach than with its potential use in the classroom. In reality the language of teaching relies far more heavily on the 'timeless' present, which expresses generalisations such as *koalas live in Australia*, or *when you boil water it becomes steam.*

A further example — most structural courses introduce the simple past tense (as in *I went, I played*) after many other grammatical items have been introduced, and yet this is what children need to be able to use as soon as possible if they are to take part in 'newstime' in their class.

It would be foolish to dismiss all such courses as worthless, since all approaches to language teaching probably have some value for some children at some times. However, a major weakness of any pre-designed language course is that it remains a matter of chance whether or not the topic and structures of the course have anything to do with the actual language skills that learners need in their regular classes. In the main, the language forms to be learned exist as autonomous objectives in the ESL class and may remain quite unrelated to learning in other parts of the curriculum. In addition, the concepts and content are often simplified to match the limited language objectives of the program, and as a result the language itself may be of little interest or use to the learners. Often there is minimal use of higher order thinking skills, leading to quite meaningless pieces of language which have no other function than to rehearse what's being learned.

Integrating language

In a more integrated approach, language objectives and content objectives compatible with each other are taught concurrently. For example, the language skills needed to talk about measurement and comparison may best be learned in a mathematics class where children are measuring each other and comparing their heights. In this situation children not only learn the appropriate language, but also have the opportunity to see how to apply this knowledge to other skills, such as transferring the information to a graph to show the comparative heights of children in the class. The integration of language and cross-curriculum content therefore can, if planned for, have the additional advantage of involving the use of higher order thinking skills. Moreover, when language and content are integrated, children have an opportunity to learn what is most relevant at that time for them to participate in class, and so can be fully engaged in learning activities and challenged at an appropriate conceptual level.

However, if such integration is to be effective, the language objectives must be carefully planned and matched with appropriate content. Providing a rich language environment is essential, but it is not enough on its own. Literature, for example, is a vital part of any language program. It provides many models of language, and a skilled teacher will draw out the personal responses which will help children to develop a life-long love of reading and good literature. But selecting themes simply on the basis that they are enjoyable, and that they allow for the use of stories, poems and songs, does not ensure that children will develop the language they need for learning in maths or science. A real danger in much so-called language integration is that the value of the literature and the integrity of the particular curriculum area can both be lost. Neither does such an approach ensure closure of the language gap which exists between competent native speakers and children learning English as a second language. Accordingly the next section will look at how language objectives can be integrated with all curriculum areas.

Programming for language across the curriculum

Identifying the functions of language

Ben, a lively ten-year-old, came running up to me and announced with delight, 'There's a huge spider over there!' He was right. It was very large. It was a whistling spider, which lives a metre under the ground and eats frogs. Fortunately this specimen was dead, safely preserved in glass in the Australian Museum. Had Ben said the same thing at a barbecue or a picnic, my reaction and the reactions of those with me would doubtless have been very different! Although the same words could be used in both situations, their function — the purpose for which they were used — would be very different. In the first case, Ben was *identifying* and *describing* what he could see. At a barbecue the words might be a *warning.*

There are many functions or purposes for which language is used in the classroom, and a useful starting point for programming for language across the curriculum is to identify the language functions which will be required through your program. This will allow you to describe in general terms the language that children will need in order to participate and to learn in your classroom. The list below represents the more common functions of language.

- agreeing and disagreeing
- apologising
- asking for permission
- asking for assistance, directions
- classifying
- comparing
- commanding/giving instructions
- criticising
- denying
- describing
- enquiring/questioning
- evaluating
- expressing likes and dislikes
- expressing position
- expressing obligation
- explaining
- hypothesising
- identifying
- inferring
- planning and predicting
- refusing
- reporting
- sequencing
- suggesting
- warning
- wishing and hoping

To identify the language functions currently being used in your own classroom, try matching some of the teaching and learning activities in your program with the relevant language functions. Look particularly at those areas of the curriculum not traditionally thought of as 'language', such as maths, science, social studies or craft. The following comments from a group of K-6 teachers may be helpful.

classifying: 'During maths activities the children were sorting shapes and talking about the groups they made.' (Kindergarten)

hypothesising: 'In social studies we were talking about the greenhouse effect, and what might happen in the future.' (Year 6)

describing: 'We were doing modelled writing and composing a setting for a story.' (Year 3)

giving and following instructions: 'In P.E. I told the children to curl up, tuck their heads in and do a forward roll.' (Year 2)

explaining: 'We've been studying rocks, and one group chose to research fossils; they gave a presentation on how fossils are formed.' (Year 5)

predicting: 'The children were discussing what we are going to see at the zoo next week and what they will need to bring on the excursion.' (Year 1)

Figure 1 (overleaf) can serve as an overview of the language used during a term. Note that it is not a student checklist and is not intended to be worked through. Neither does it imply that a particular function is 'completed'. Rather it can be used as an ongoing record to help ensure that classroom activities allow for an appropriate range of language. Checking that you are using a range of language functions throughout the program will help ensure that you give learners opportunities to hear and use a variety of language.

Choosing the words

Within any of the language functions there are many ways of expressing a similar idea. Think, for example, of how you might express, as part of an explanation, the cause and effect relationship between these two ideas:

It rained.   The soil got washed away.

Any competent native speaker could offer a range of alternative wordings, such as:

It rained and so the soil got washed away.

The soil got washed away because it rained.

Because it rained the soil got washed away.

As a result of the rain, the soil got washed away.

The soil was eroded as a result of the rain.

The soil getting washed away was the result of the rain.

The rain caused the soil to be washed away.

The soil erosion was caused by rain.

Each of these wordings represents a different way of expressing a similar idea, but each change of wording also changes the meaning slightly because it gives a different focus to the idea. For example, beginning with *The soil* has a different emphasis to beginning with *The rain* or *As a result of*. The wordings also vary in complexity — some, such as the first example, being very simple, while the later examples involve the more complex use of language associated with written texts.

Part of programming for language across the curriculum includes making decisions about the sorts of wordings (or, as they are usually called, structures or sentence patterns) that are likely to occur through teacher modelling and group activities. Of course it is impossible to accurately predict language use, and if we were to restrict ourselves to previously planned wordings, our language use would certainly sound quite unlike authentic language. Neither of course is it possible or

WEEK	classifying	comparing	giving/following instructions	describing	questioning	evaluating	expressing position	explaining	hypothesising	planning/predicting	reporting	sequencing	others
1													
2													
3													
4													
5													
6													
7													
8													
9													
10													
11													
12													
13													

N.B.   'Social' use of language in the classroom includes: asking permission, asking assistance, asking directions, denying, promising, requesting, suggesting, wishing and hoping.

Figure 1: An Overview of Language Functions

even desirable to restrict children to using set phrases and predetermined language within a particular learning activity.

However, it is important to give some consideration to what kind of language is appropriate for a particular activity, and for a particular grade. It is especially important where there are large numbers of second language speakers because of the tendency many language learners have to 'stay with the known'.

This is a strategy with which you will be familiar if you have ever visited a country where you do not speak the language. You will probably find out one way of asking directions, one way of greeting people, one way of asking for what you want in a shop, and so on. Unless you have reason to do so, you may well not venture outside this known language. If what you have learned to say works for you and allows you to meet your immediate needs, then it is often easier to stay with the known. You avoid attempting a more complex wording because you can manage without it. You also make fewer mistakes if you use only familiar language. However, as the examples above show, different wordings produce different meanings, and so if the range of wordings you are able to produce is restricted, the range of meanings will also be reduced.

Remaining with the known, therefore, while it may be useful for the tourist, is a hazardous strategy for the bilingual learner in school. A child may, for example, be able to understand and produce a structure like: *The soil got washed away because it rained*. But at some stage in school he or she will need to understand and use a more complex structure such as: *The soil erosion was caused by rain*. Without the word *erosion* to 'label' the concept, the child will neither have the means to recognise and learn the concept, nor be able to relate it to other ideas such as: *Soil erosion is a great problem in Australia*. Many abstract concepts like this cannot be developed from personal and concrete experience alone, and language itself is the means whereby children learn to recognise and name more abstract ideas. If there is a gap in a learner's language resources, then the thinking processes that are dependent on them will also be restricted. This is particularly true of second language learners whose early switch to English has prevented them from developing concepts in their first language.

Whereas a competent native speaker will have a considerable 'language pool' from which to create and choose meaning, a second language learner may know only one way of saying something in English and so be restricted in the choice of meaning. Many children may in fact have quite limited English language resources, but because what they say or write is grammatically correct, their difficulties may not be noticed.

Extending the language — comprehensible input plus!

An important concept in language acquisition is the notion of the learner needing to hear models of language which are *comprehensible* but also *beyond what the learners are able to produce themselves.*

There are many ways of making language comprehensible in the classroom — through using concrete materials, for instance, or diagrams, charts, graphs and illustrations, or through drama or mime activities. And it is worth remembering that learners' understanding of language is always far ahead of what they can produce themselves. But it is also important to provide the child with new language to use. That is why it is important that the teaching program includes reference to the language structures that will be integral to the particular unit of work. Unless children are given access, through teacher or peer modelling, to the language that they cannot yet control, we cannot be sure that the language used by a Year 6 child will be much different from that used by a Year 1 child.

In a school with large numbers of migrant children, the notion of access to new language is particularly important. In such a school it is very easy to fall into the habit of constantly simplifying our language because we expect not to be understood. But if we only ever use basic language such as *put in* or *take out* or *go faster*, some children will not have any opportunity to learn other ways of expressing these ideas, such as *insert* or *remove* or *accelerate*. And these are the words which are needed to refer to the general concepts related to the ideas, such as *removal, insertion* and *acceleration*.

In programming for language, then, we must aim not only to make language comprehensible, but also to demonstrate, through modelling, new ways of expressing ideas. In all language learning learners must have constant demonstrations of the language in use, and these demonstrations must include new language which they are not yet able to produce by themselves.

A language framework for programming

Most teachers have a way of programming which suits them. The framework suggested opposite in Figure 2 (an example filled in for Kindergarten/Year 1 children) is not in itself a programming format, but if you use it beside your own program, it can help to set language objectives in any curriculum area. The language objectives are expressed in terms of functions, and structures or sentence patterns as described earlier in this chapter.

Column 2 of the framework refers to the classroom activities that children will be engaged in while they explore the topic. These will require certain functions of language which are listed in column 3. (Compare the list given on p. 14.) Column 4 relates to the specific sentence patterns, or language structures, which are related to these functions. This is the language that the teacher will *consciously model* and that the children will have opportunity to use. The final column refers to any specific vocabulary associated with the unit (such as *marsupial, mammal, pouch, kangaroo, monotreme* in a topic about Australian animals) and also vocabulary items which will extend children's concepts and language (e.g. go faster - *accelerate*).

Planning for language within a framework like this means that you will be teaching, in an integrated way, the language which is necessary for understanding and talking about curriculum content, and giving children opportunity for developing language in a relevant and meaningful context. In the program a language framework may accompany the unit of work as a whole, or reference to the functions and structures may be included throughout the program. What is

TOPIC	ACTIVITIES	LANGUAGE FUNCTIONS	LANGUAGE STRUCTURES	VOCABULARY
Shape / Size / Colour	arranging attribute blocks (as a matrix or in sets)	classifying	they are all (blue) these are all (triangles)	triangle square circle
	barrier game: giving partner instructions	{ giving instructions { describing position	draw a ... colour it ... draw a triangle under the... beside the... between the...	red green blue
	'What's Missing?' game △ ○ □ (blue) △ ○ □ (green) △ □ (red) (use large and small blocks to extend matrix)	describing	it's a big, red circle (order of adjectives)	under beside between

The topic ...   includes these activities ... which require these language functions ...   which will be modelled using this language.

Figure 2: Language Framework

important is that you make conscious decisions about the language objectives of your program and that you are able to answer the question: *What is the language that I want children to be able to use by the end of this unit?*

How do I decide which language to select as a focus?

Decisions about what language to focus on within a unit of work need to take into account two questions:

- What are the language demands of the curriculum?
- What are the language needs of the children?

So far this chapter has focused on the first of these and has shown how programming for language across the curriculum involves looking at a unit of work and deciding which language functions and structures will become the language objectives.

However, it is also important to consider the language needs of the children and relate them to the program. Instead of always allowing the content to dictate the language, we also need to select content, or adapt or add activities within a unit of work, on the basis of the language children will need to learn. Here are two examples of how language needs may suggest content or activities.

1 Many bilingual children, particularly younger children, have difficulty in expressing position in English, confusing words like *in, on, under, beside, between, at the back of* and so on. An appropriate choice of literature would include a deliberate selection of books in which these words are used and their meaning made clear through the context, or through clear and text-supportive illustrations (such as those in Pat Hutchins' *Rosie's Walk*). It would also be possible to focus on these words through P.E. activities, through some maths activities, and through communicative barrier games, which can be linked with any area of the curriculum. (For a description and examples of barrier games, see Chapter 3.)

2 Many second language learners have difficulty in expressing degrees of obligation in English — with words such as *must, may, might, could, should, ought to, mustn't*, etc. A choice of topic involving, for example, the discussion and creation of a set of class rules, or a unit on safety, would be suitable vehicles for modelling and using this language.

Taking language and learning needs rather than content as a starting point gives you the flexibility to design a program which is appropriate and relevant to the children. The curriculum is fitted to the child instead of the child being expected to fit the curriculum! Of course there will be certain content which you feel is so important that all children should cover it. But the feeling that content must be 'covered' at all costs often leads to feelings of pressure and frustration in classes where many children do not have adequate English language skills to cope. An easy solution is to simplify and water down the program, yet this is a 'bandaid' approach which offers no guarantee that bilingual children will eventually develop the necessary language skills. It is easy to neglect the fact that it is the acquisition of thinking and language skills which gives children the capacity to become independent learners. Taking time to focus on language in all curriculum areas is time well spent, because developing effective language skills allows children to go on being learners long after the 'facts' within a particular unit may have been forgotten. They will have 'learned to learn'. Thus, where there are large classes of bilingual children, it is important that content and themes are partly selected on the basis of the skills and language children need to acquire, and the opportunities they provide for problem solving and collaborative tasks.

Assessing language needs

If a knowledge of children's language needs is to influence the program, then how do we find out what they are? Assessment in its broadest sense involves considering attitudes, processes, skills and products. It occurs when we observe children, when we interact with children, and when we analyse their language.

Analysis of the language use of children learning English as a second language is vital if we are to make programming decisions which will meet their language needs. Any effective language program takes as its starting point the existing language competencies of the child, and works towards developing the language which the child still needs to acquire. The same principle underpins a good ESL program. We need information about the language areas and structures in which a child needs support before making final programming decisions about which language areas to focus on and what strategies we might use to do this. Chapters 4 and 9, which deal with the development and assessment of spoken and written language, give examples of ways of analysing language to identify areas of need.

Figure 3, over the page, illustrates the relationship suggested here between the learning needs, the curriculum and the program.

Modelling through questioning

The questions teachers ask are an important way to create the situations where certain language patterns are likely to occur. The language structures within the questions themselves will often model the language which learners will need to use during discussion, and in answering the questions.

It is also important that children have opportunities to ask questions — of each other and of the teacher. At the beginning of a topic or experiment, for example, they could pose questions about what they would like to find out, suggesting possible research questions for the whole class or planning individual projects in question form. Helping children to develop questioning techniques and the language structures of a variety of questions moves them towards becoming independent learners. Being able to ask appropriate questions will help them to access or clarify information, and to think critically and laterally.

The following examples of question types may be useful for reference as you are programming and planning classroom activities, especially those which involve

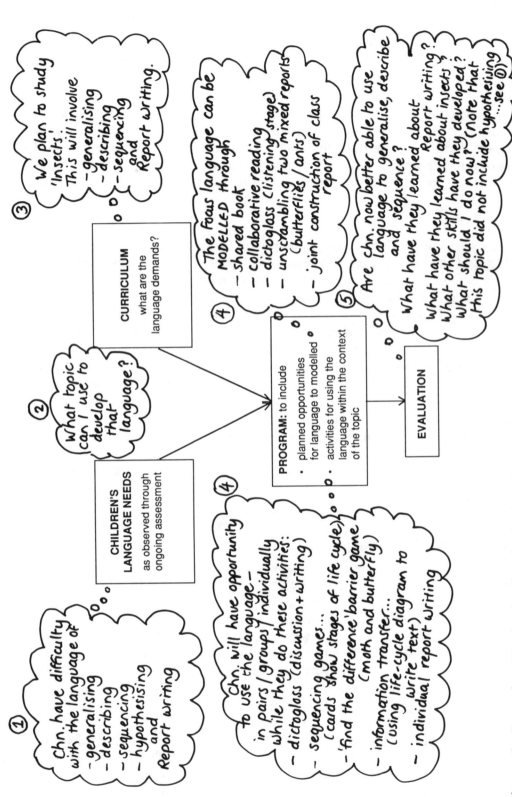

Figure 3: Learning Needs, the Curriculum and the Program

spoken language. (You will find that in some cases the questions could be included in more than one category.)

Classifying

Which of these go together? Why?

Can any of these be put together?

How are these things alike/similar/different?

What could you call these groups?

What are the characteristics of all the things in this group?

What criteria have been used to classify these?

How could you rearrange ...?

How could you compare ... and ...?

Can you find another way to ...?

Describing

What is ... like?

What can you see?

What did you notice about ...?

How would you describe ...?

Evaluating

Do you think this is a good thing/bad thing? Why?

Do you agree with this? Why?

How do you feel about this? Why?

Is there anything you would have done differently? Why?

Why was this done? Do you think it was a good idea?

What were the reasons for this?

Do you think this is just/fair/appropriate? Why?

What do you think is important about this? Why?

How could this be improved?

How could you justify this?

Can you take another point of view about ...?

How would you feel if you were ...?

Is this the best way to ...?

Explaining

Why does ...?

How do you ...?

Why did this happen?

Why do you think that ...?

What caused this?

What might be the result of ...? Why do you think so?

Can anyone think of another reason/explanation?

Can you explain ...?

Generalising

What is true about all of these?

What can you tell us about ...?

What have you found out about ...?

What seems to be generally true about ...?

What have you learned about ...?

What conclusions can you draw now?

What does this tell you about ...?

Inferring

Can you explain from this how ...?/why ...?

What do you think might be happening here? Why?

What do you think might cause this?

Why do you think they did this?

How do you imagine they are feeling?

Can anyone think of a different idea?

Predicting and hypothesising

What are we going to see at ...?

What would/might happen if ...?

If . . . , what do you think will be the result?

What would it be like if ...?

What would you do if ...?

How would you plan for ...?

Recalling information

How many ...?

Where is ...?

In which year did ...?

Why did ...?

A checklist for programming

The following checklist is to help you ensure that the needs of the second language learner are being met.

In your classroom ...

- Is there a comfortable and stress-free environment?

- Is language being used purposefully, for real learning tasks?

- Do learning activities allow for a range of language functions?

- Do you have language objectives in all curriculum areas?

- Do these reflect the learning needs of the children?

- Is the language you use comprehensible?

- Does the language you use sufficiently extend and challenge the children?

- Are children given an opportunity in learning activities to *use* language which has been modelled?

- Are children given opportunities to use language with different audiences — with each other, with teachers, with other adults?

- Are children encouraged and given opportunities to work with peers in problem solving and collaborative learning situations?

- Does the classroom organisation (e.g. types of groupings) give bilingual learners adequate support in all learning tasks?

- Is the first language of children clearly acknowledged?

- Are the resources to be used within the capabilities of the children?

- Are your expectations of the learning outcomes for bilingual children sufficiently high?

- If there is an ESL teacher in the school, has there been consultation or joint planning of the program?

CHAPTER THREE

An Interactive Classroom: Developing Spoken Language

Proficiency in spoken language is essential if children are to achieve their potential at school. This chapter will illustrate some of the ways in which oral language development is linked to literacy development and to the processes of thinking and learning, and offer some suggestions for promoting the use of oral language within the classroom.

All research into language development, including studies in both first and second language acquisition, support the notion of language *use* as a major principle for language *development*. Being immersed in language and having access to good language models is of course important, but it is not in itself sufficient to develop language competence. Children who spend a large part of their waking hours in front of a television, for example, may be receiving — depending on the quality of the program — good models of language, but this exposure will not be enough to develop their language. Children also need to *use* language in interaction with other children and adults.

If you have listened to young children developing their first language, you will be aware of how talk (particularly talk with a more competent language user) helps them to experiment with new language forms and develop new ways of formulating and linking ideas. Likewise, children learning English as a second language need many opportunities to use spoken language, and so oral language activities in the classroom are of special importance. Such situations provide an opportunity for second language learners to interact with more competent speakers of the language, and to develop their own language skills through hearing good models and by using the language purposefully themselves.

Jim Cummins (1988), who has researched the language development of children learning a second language at school, has emphasised the importance of an 'interactive' classroom. This is a classroom which is not teacher-centred and where there is scope for genuine dialogue between students and between teacher and students.

This kind of classroom not only supports one of the major principles of language development (that of language use), but also creates opportunities for children to be active in their own learning. This is particularly important for children who are less familiar with the language and culture of schooling. In a very teacher-centred classroom these children may 'learn to fail' simply because they are continually expected to play a passive role and have very few opportunities to participate successfully. Some learning difficulties may themselves be the result of this culture of 'learned helplessness'. There is now considerable research to suggest that a major factor in the academic success of linguistic minority groups is the degree to which learning takes place in an interactive rather than a passive environment (Skutnabb-Kangas & Cummins 1988).

Talking while doing

It is through talk that much learning occurs. Talk allows children to think aloud, to formulate ideas, to set up and evaluate hypotheses and to reach tentative decisions in a context that is not restricted by the more formal demands of written language. To see this happening, let's look at part of a discussion between two Year 4 children. Both speak another language at home.

Patrick and Joseph have been given the task of designing a zoo enclosure to suit a particular Australian animal. (The class had previously studied a number of native animals and had each written a report about the animal of their choice.) Patrick and Joseph have chosen to design a habitat for a platypus, and here they are deciding whether it will be necessary to build a wall around their enclosure.

> *P*: this is going to be like the back and this is going to be ... the front ... no he won't ... he wouldn't wander around the water and go out there so we don't need a gate there because he won't wander that far out
>
> *J*: and the trees would ... these trees ...
>
> *P*: right
>
> *J*: so ... if we have a sign that says ... if you find a platypus take it ... take him to ... a ... no ... a staff member

P: no no ... don't touch it ... please do not touch ... yes yes that's what we'll do ... we'll put ... please don't ... no ... please don't touch platypus spine ...

J: no ... what is it? ... what is it? ... it's got something that's poisonous

P: so that'll make the people walk away ... because they aren't going to take it home if it's got something poisonous on it

J: please ... please don't touch the platypus because it has ... a poisonous *spur*

P: yes ... please do not touch the platypus because of its spur ... its spur is dangerous and you will have to be taken to hospital ... right?

In this text language is being used to offer possible solutions to a problem and to clarify ideas. The children are also reflecting on past learning (note the attempt to recall the word *spur*). The text shows how the two speakers use language collaboratively to negotiate a shared meaning. Through their successful negotiation they produce a final wording for their notice which incorporates the earlier suggestions of both children. It is quite likely that neither child would have come to this final version alone. It is also striking how full of conditional language and explanations this short dialogue is, and correspondingly how much richer it seems than the language typically produced by children in a teacher-dominated classroom.

If children are to 'learn by talking', then we must also create classroom situations where they have opportunities to be confronted by viewpoints not necessarily their own and discuss possible solutions to a problem with their peers or with adults. Let's return to Patrick and Joseph for an example. While they are making a list of what will be necessary for their enclosure, some disagreement develops about the function and necessity for a dam.

P: it needs a dam at the end

J: but ...

P: well where does it end then ... you've got to have a dam to end

J: not ... can't you just do a little ... just like a dead end to the stream?

P: that *is* a dead end ... that's a dam ... everything needs a dam

J: Patrick ... Patrick ... the water just stops ... all around there ... that's just sand ... the water stops there

P: I know ... it stops just there ... yeah ... like ... that's what a dam *is* ... every creek needs a dam

J: it just goes up onto the bank

P: it's not like the beach ... it's not a stream ... it's a creek

J: it just goes up into the shore

P: they need dams don't they? ... every creek needs a dam ... otherwise it would just run up on shore and get all the trees out

J: it just goes up into ...

P: if it does it's going to take away the dirt every time and pull back the dirt and then the trees will be just falling in the creek

J: it's not like the sea Patrick ... it doesn't go in waves

P: but when he swims in there he's going to make waves

J: he's not that powerful

P: well he moves doesn't he?

J: when you're in a pool ... do you ever see ... big waves when you're swimming?

P: yeah

J: going up? ... going up into the grass and ... whoosh?

P: yeah ... when I do bombs anyway ... go on write down *dam* ... what else does he need?

J: how do you spell enclosure?

In order to resolve disagreement, speakers must not only justify their own position, but listen to and either accommodate or refute their opponent's. In a whole class discussion it is likely that the teacher will take responsibility for holding the discussion together, indicating who may speak and, since he or she has control of the turn-taking, also probably for how long. In a two-person dialogue there is far more opportunity for both speakers to engage in a piece of connected and cohesive discourse, to alternately take the roles of speaker and listener and to use language to challenge and clarify thinking. Patrick claims that a creek must end in a dam, and offers as justification his notion that the water would otherwise erode the bank and cause the trees to fall down. Joseph claims that the water 'just stops', and that since there will be no waves a dam is not necessary. These are quite abstract ideas, and although at this point the children had not reached agreement (and had failed to recognise that streams do not 'end' at all), both had had an opportunity to articulate and clarify their own thinking and to respond to their partner's ideas.

These texts also illustrate how much the learning depends upon the personal involvement of the learner. What is being learned is both language and knowledge. Knowledge is not simply a 'preformulated' product passed on from teacher, but is being reconstructed by the two children during the course of the interaction.

Although thought and language are not the same thing, they are interdependent, and language provides a way of reflecting on thought processes and of stating them explicitly. Such control is essential for learning. A major role for classroom teachers, particularly where their students may not be competent in the language of the school, is to encourage the use of language for conceptual learning. If we wish to give children the opportunity to learn through the use of spoken language, and at the same time to increase the control of language itself, then we must regularly set up small-group, task-oriented situations in which children have direction and purpose for their talk, and in which those who are less competent in the language have opportunities to interact with those who are more proficient.

Reporting back — a strategy for language development

How does oral language development relate to and influence literacy development? Vygotsky (1962) has suggested that it is the abstract quality of written language rather than the 'mechanics' of reading that causes difficulties for some children. To read with meaning requires an understanding of words and grammatical forms which are often quite different from those encountered in everyday chat about concrete experiences, or from the sort of language that children may use while they are engaged in 'hands-on' activities.

To become more aware of these differences, let's look at a series of four texts. The first, a spoken text, was produced by two nine-year-olds.

> TEXT 1
>
> try this one ... no it doesn't go ... it doesn't move ... try that ... yes ... it does a bit ... that won't work ... it's not metal ... these are the best ... it's making them go really fast.

The language in this text is 'context-bound', meaning that it is very dependent on what is happening in the immediate situation. It is unlikely that it could be understood on its own by anyone who was not actually present and able to see what *this one*, *it* and *that* referred to. In fact the children who produced this text were experimenting with a magnet and finding out which things were attracted to it.

After the hands-on experience, the children were asked to report back to the class about what they had discovered. They now had to be conscious of the needs of their listeners, who did not have the benefit of a visual context. Their language had to make everything explicit, as Text 2 shows.

> TEXT 2
>
> We tried a pin, a pencil sharpener, some iron filings and a piece of plastic. The magnet didn't attract the pin, but it did attract the pencil sharpener and the iron filings. It didn't attract the plastic.

This second piece of spoken language is much more like written language because it begins to create its own context. The objects and processes are named (e.g. *pin, pencil sharpener, iron filings, attract*), and so we do not need the visual clues to make it comprehensible. However, it is still dependent on the audience's understanding of the total context — that is, that the speakers had been engaged in a classroom activity which involved a science experiment.

The children then wrote about their experiment, and Text 3 is an example of one of these pieces of writing.

TEXT 3

Our experiment was to find out what a magnet attracted. We discovered that a magnet attracts some kinds of metal. It attracted the iron filings, but not the pin. It also did not attract things that were not metal.

Here the text is far more complete. It creates its own context and makes the whole situation explicit to the reader. This includes the opening which sets the scene (*Our experiment was to find out ...*). In this piece, as in the other texts, the writer refers mainly to the particular experiment she has taken part in, but she also generalises from the experience (*a magnet attracts some kinds of metal*).

The final text is taken from a children's encyclopedia. There is now no reference to a specific event; the information is given through generalisations.

TEXT 4

A magnet is a piece of metal which is surrounded by an invisible field of force which affects any magnetic material within it. It is able to pick up a piece of steel or iron because its magnetic field flows into the metal, turning it into a temporary magnet.

Setting up reporting-back situations in any curriculum area (as in Text 2) is a very practical way of giving children practice and opportunity to hear and use language at a more abstract level, as well as giving them a reason to reflect on and clarify their own new learning. For while hands-on experiences are a very valuable starting point for language development, they do not, on their own, offer children adequate opportunities to develop the more 'context-free' language associated with reading and writing. As the four examples show, a reporting-back situation is a bridge into the more formal demands of literacy. It allows children to try out in speech — in a realistic and authentic situation — the sort of language that they will meet in books and which they need to develop in their writing. Where children's own language background has not led to this extension of oral language, it becomes even more important for the classroom to provide such opportunities.

Thinking of classroom language as a continuum, as shown by the four texts, is a helpful way of identifying those language areas that children are most likely to have difficulty with. The closer that language is in terms of time or physical space to the 'original' context (Text 1), the more is it possible for the speaker to rely on the concrete and visual surroundings and the less is *language* needed. The further away it is (Texts 2, 3, 4), the greater become the language demands and the more is required of the speaker's linguistic resources. As the examples show, the more 'removed' texts involve the use of words and grammatical forms which are different from everyday chat or the sort of language that may be used during hands-on activities.

Language development can in part be measured by a child's increasing ability to separate language from a concrete experience and reconstruct the experience (in a different place and at a different time) through the use of language alone. This is what any adult has observed who has talked with very young children learning their first language! It is only as a child's speech begins to mature that there is sufficient information *within the language* for the meaning to be understood by someone who did not share in the particular experience. Similarly children learning English as a second language may have few difficulties with producing something like Text 1, because they can rely on the visual context to make their meaning clear and do not need the specific vocabulary associated with the topic, but they will probably find it far more difficult to produce something like Texts 2 and 3. So just because children are fluent in a situation like that of Text 1, we cannot assume that they will automatically be able to write about what they have experienced.

There will be many opportunities within your regular teaching program to set up situations for the development of spoken language. Try looking to see where there is already scope for oral language activities, both *talk while doing* and *reporting back*. Below are some examples of the sorts of activities that may be a regular part of your program, and which relate to some of the more common functions of oral language in a range of curriculum areas. The list of question types in Chapter 2 may also suggest ideas for setting up oral language situations.

Giving an opinion or personal response

- responding to a book
- responding to a news event
- offering a personal opinion about a current event (e.g. environmental issues)
- evaluating events/behaviour/character within a novel.

Narrating

- recounting a personal experience (newstime)
- retelling a narrative
- telling a joke.

Describing people and things, describing position

- barrier games (see next section)
- maths activities involving position (e.g. explaining where to put things)
- describing a person to someone else (e.g. in literature: a character in a story, a person in a wanted poster or an 'identikit' picture)

Nancy and Marco talk through a maths problem (above), *and Nancy reports back how they solved it* (below).

- describing known people (e.g. in social studies units such as *Me* or *Our Community:* describing oneself, a child in the class, people in the community)

- describing a picture or a setting in a story

- describing what something looks like (e.g. in music: an unusual musical instrument).

Giving instructions, describing a process

- telling someone how to make something (e.g. in craft, cooking)

- telling someone how to play a game (e.g. in P.E., or a board game)

- explaining how something works (e.g. a computer)

- describing a natural process (e.g. how a fossil is formed, the process of erosion, the life cycle of an insect)

- describing how something is made (e.g. stages in the manufacture of an item)

- describing how something is done (e.g. coal or mineral mining).

Giving an explanation

- explaining why something occurs (e.g. in science: why boats float, why it rains)

- discussing and explaining reasons (e.g. in social studies: why particular rules exist in society, at school)

- explaining why a particular solution to a problem has been chosen (e.g. problem solving in maths, moral dilemmas, rank-ordering activities).

Presenting and supporting an argument

- small group discussions relating to current issues

- formal debates

- 'simulation' computer games which involve group decision making.

Hypothesising

- hands-on science experiments and problem-solving situations (e.g. those which pose the question *what do you think will happen if ...?*)

- maths and computer activities which involve problem solving

- discussions and games which require projection into the unknown (e.g. *what would happen if cars were banned? what might Australia be like in 2020?*).

More ideas for games and activities

The following suggestions may act as a springboard for other ideas. All the games and activities suggested here are communicative: that is, there is a genuine need to use language in order to get something done. The aim is to create a situation where there is reason, opportunity and a purpose for using language. Often this may involve the use of a particular language function, such as asking questions or giving instructions. In communicative activities something *happens* as a result of the language being used. There is an outcome, such as the solving of a problem or the sharing of information. A key element in many of the games is the conveying of information — one of the two (or more) players must be in a state of ignorance. When a game is first played, the teacher is the 'information possessor' and the children are the 'information seekers', but once the game is known, it is important that the children have opportunities to play both roles.

Some types of activities

Problem-solving activities

Groups of children must solve a problem by consensus. Many maths activities lend themselves to this. Simulation computer games (such as *Settlement*, Elizabeth Computer Centre, Tasmania) are ideal, when played in small groups, for generating discussion. Many of the games described below involve the solving of a problem, such as Game 4 (map game 2), where children must complete an incomplete map, or Game 11, where children must decide on a rank order.

Information-sharing activities

Each child within the group holds part of the information required to complete the task. They take turns in sharing their information. The group then decides how to interpret the information as a whole. As examples, see Games 7 and 8.

Rank-ordering activities

Children consider priorities for ordering given information. Final ranking involves reaching a consensus of opinion. As an example, see Game 11.

Enquiry and elimination activities

Children need to elicit information from one of their group through questioning and then eliminate irrelevant information in order to solve the problem. As an example, see Game 10.

Barrier games

The barrier in these games may be physical, such as a sheet of cardboard between the two children, but the children may simply sit back to back. Child A has a complete set of information which Child B needs in order to complete the task. Or Child A may give the relevant information to Child B. As examples, see Games 1–4.

Matrix activities

A matrix is a way of organising information. Matrices can be used in a wide range of communicative activities involving listening, speaking, reading and writing. Any activity which involves transferring or interpreting information from one form (such as a matrix) to another (such as a piece of written text) is a useful language activity.

Some examples of communicative games and activities

These games are best introduced by the teacher playing with a pair of children or with a group, or by two teachers demonstrating the game to the class. This gives an opportunity for the particular language of the game to be modelled.

The games are intended to be used as part of regular small group or pair activities. As far as possible provide at least one good language model within the group, or as one of the pair. Where there is an appropriate language partner, many of the games can be played with new arrival children using their first language, before they begin to attempt to play the game in English.

1 Describe and Draw (barrier game)

You need two sheets of paper and pencils and textas. A describes to B what he or she has drawn (or is drawing). B reproduces the drawing according to A's description. The drawings may be of real objects or shapes, such as triangles or squares.

possible language: describing position (*beside, next to, under, on the left of, on the right of, draw a, put the*)

2 Describe and Arrange (barrier game)

You need two identical sets of pictures: for example, two sets of houses, two sets of cars, or two sets of butterflies. A describes to B how to arrange them on a grid. If some of the pictures are very similar, the children will need to describe them clearly and in detail in order to distinguish them.

possible language: as for Game 1; also describing (*put the one with the red spots next to the blue and red one with pointed wings*)

3 Find the Difference (barrier game)

You need two pictures, like those on p. 47, which are identical except for a number of minor differences. (Draw a simple picture, photocopy it, and make the minor changes by using white-out on the copy and then redrawing. Finally photocopy both versions.) The task for the children is to find the differences. They may ask questions or describe their own picture. They should be told how many differences there are.

possible language: questioning (*have you got a ...? is the boy ...?*); describing (*the boy with spiky hair*); expressing position (*next to the boy on the floor, just under the window*)

4 Map Game 1 (barrier game)

You need two identical maps. A directs B from an agreed starting point to a destination which is unknown to B.

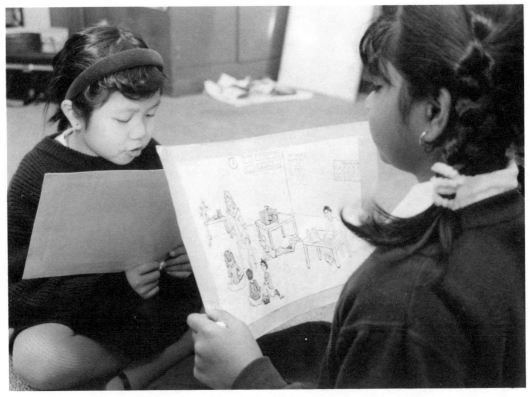

Sharon and Madhushini are developing their English skills as they play a 'Find the Difference' barrier game.

possible language: giving directions (*go along X Street, cross over the second road and then turn left*)

4 Map Game 2 *(barrier game)*

You need two maps of the same area with incomplete information about names of streets and buildings. Map A has different information from Map B, but together they give all the information. The task is to complete both maps by sharing information.

possible language: asking questions (*what's the name of the building opposite the post office?*); expressing position (*opposite, beside, around the corner from*)

5 Find My Partner *(group game, four to six children)*

You need four to six pictures, depending on how many children are playing. Two of the pictures are identical, but the others have minor differences (see overleaf). One of the two identical pictures is marked with a cross or with 'Find my partner'. The child who gets this card must find the partner by questioning other members of the group.

possible language: questioning (*has your cat got ...?*); describing (*this one's got a stripey tail*)

6 *Kim's Game* (*group game*)

You need a selection of real objects which can be placed on a table. Children look at them for a few minutes and then the objects are covered with a cloth. Children attempt to remember them.

possible language: names of objects; describing (*a cup with a broken handle*)

7 *Jigsaw Pictures* (*group game*)

You need four or five magazine pictures, depending on how many children are going to play. Cut each picture into five or six pieces, in such a way as to make clear what the adjoining piece might look like or contain. Label the back of one piece from each picture with a cross. Shuffle and deal the pieces to the children, ensuring that each child has one piece with a cross. This identifies which picture that child is to make. Without showing their pieces to the group, the children must each reconstruct their own picture by taking it in turns to ask anyone in the group for the pieces they need.

possible language: questioning (*have you got a piece with …?*); describing (*a piece with green leaves and sky on it*)

8 *Make a Story* (*group game*)

You need four to six pictures which tell a predictable story. Give one picture to each child, who must not show it to the rest of the group. Each child describes his or her picture, and the group works out a possible order for the story.

possible language: describing people and processes (*there's a boy looking at a monster in a cage, the monster is bending the bars*); **ordinal** numbers (*this one must go second*)

9 Classification Game (*group game*)

You need a set of cards showing a variety of animals or objects. The group must classify them in as many ways as possible. There are no right or wrong answers as long as appropriate reasons are given. (One group of enterprising teachers on an inservice classified the animals shown in the example below into hors d'oeuvres and main courses!)

possible language: classifying and giving reasons (*these go together because they are all insects, the fish and the crab both live in the sea, the spider and the crab both have eight legs*)

10 Guess the Animal *(enquiry and elimination group game)*

Choose a large picture showing a range of members within a set — for example, a picture showing many different kinds of animals. One member of the group silently chooses an animal and the others must guess which one it is by asking *yes/no* questions only. Restricting the number of questions the group can ask encourages the children to ask questions which will elicit the maximum amount of information. For example, the answer *yes* to the question *does it live on land?* will allow the elimination of all animals which live in water. With younger children it may be necessary to cover up with blank cards what has been eliminated.

Many large pictures can be exploited in a similar way: for example, a picture of a room in which children must find the missing dollar.

possible language: names of animals/objects; questioning and generalising (*does it live in water?*)

11 Desert Island Game *(rank-ordering group game)*

In groups the children must decide, perhaps from a given list, what would be most useful to have if they were shipwrecked on an island.

possible language: expressing the conditional (*if we take this we'll ..., if we had this we would ...*); comparing and giving reasons (*the knife would be more useful because ...*)

12 The Gift Game *(group game)*

You need a sheet of cardboard and a selection of small pictures of objects. Junk mail advertising catalogues are ideal! Make a game board with the pictures stuck around the edge of the cardboard. These represent 'gifts', so be creative and include a range of things from pens to yachts, plus a few bizarre items such as castor oil or zinc cream. On small cards write some characters: e.g. your best friend, your teacher, a three-day-old baby, a rich uncle who has everything, an eighty-year-old, etc.

Each member of the group is dealt three or four character cards. In turn they throw a die, and as they land on a 'gift', they must justify the choice of that gift to one of their characters. The group must decide if it is an appropriate gift. If they decide it is, the player discards the character card. The first person to have discarded all his or her character cards is the winner. This is a lively game and gives great opportunity for imagination.

possible language: giving reasons (*I'm going to give the blender to an eighty-year-old because he hasn't got any teeth*); disagreeing (*I don't think that's a very suitable gift because ...*)

13 Collaborative Crossword Puzzle *(barrier game)*

Both children have the same basic crossword. The clues have not been given, but all the 'down' words have been filled in on one crossword and all the 'across' words on the other. Working collaboratively, the children must both complete their own crossword from clues made up by their partner. They must not say or spell the words.

possible language: vocabulary related to theme or topic work; definitions (*this is* *something which* ...); describing (*it has six legs and three parts to its body, it is used for* ..., *it can/is able to* ...)

A checklist for selecting communicative activities

To decide how useful an activity may be, consider to what extent you could answer *yes* to the following questions.

- Is talking *necessary?*
- Is interaction *necessary?*
- Are content areas of the curriculum being reinforced?
- Is at least one child using 'stretches' of language?
- Is thinking involved?
- Is the pace right, with enough variety within a given time span?
- Are all children in a group involved, either in speaking or in listening?

— CHAPTER FOUR —

Assessing Spoken Language

Spoken language shares some features in common with written language, but in many ways it is very different (Halliday 1985). So before considering how we might assess it, it will be useful to look at the features of spoken language. (It may also be helpful at this point to turn back to the spoken texts of Patrick and Joseph in the previous chapter.)

Spoken language is contextual. Like written language it functions differently in different situations, and it will be influenced by elements within each situation. These include the topic, the relationships of the speakers, whether or not the speakers are in visual contact, and whether or not the talk refers to the immediate context that the speakers are in. (To see how language varies in this way, refer back to the example of the science texts on pp. 30-31.)

It is purposeful. Like all language it has a purpose. It may involve getting someone to do something, such as a request to open the window. Or it may involve an exchange of information, such as telling a listener about something.

It is unpredictable and spontaneous. Speakers do not normally know in advance exactly what response they will receive, nor how the discourse will develop. Unrehearsed speech is a process of negotiation of meanings between speaker and listener. If the process is not to break down, they need to share understandings. What each speaker says is dependent for its meaning on what has already occurred and will in turn provide the linguistic context for what will follow.

It involves interactive strategies. These include feedback to the speaker and clarification sequences. Such sequences occur, for example, when the speaker recognises that the listener has not understood, or the listener asks for clarification.

Traditional assessment techniques in language often focused on a particular linguistic item, such as the past tense *-ed* ending. Or they may have focused on a range of skills simultaneously, as in a dictation. In either case language knowledge was usually considered in isolation from real contexts. The interactive processes involved in translating this knowledge into actual language behaviour were often ignored. (This is apparent when children who score high marks in a spelling test fail to carry over this knowledge into actual writing tasks.)

The purpose of ongoing assessment is to give teachers information about children's strengths and areas of difficulty. Good assessment procedures give teachers specific information which will be helpful in planning future learning activities. To do this, however, an assessment procedure needs to be based in a context which is realistic for the learner. At school and in relation to spoken language, this means real oral and interactive classroom situations, where the language is not 'rehearsed' but reflects the particular features of speech described above.

Considering assessment in this way means that it is neither an extra to the curriculum, nor something additional to be fitted into an already busy timetable. Since the process of assessment should model good teaching practice, any of the strategies, games and activities described in the previous chapter could also be situations in which spoken language is assessed. The following are some criteria to help in selecting the kinds of situations which are likely to give you the most information.

☐ Choose tasks which are part of normal school activities and familiar to the children.

☐ Over the year use a range of situations which have different purposes and therefore make different language demands on the speakers. Retelling a story and describing a science experiment, for example, would require speakers to use different areas of the language system. (See the examples of spoken language situations on pp. 32-34, or the list of language functions on p. 14.)

☐ Where possible, choose situations in which children are interacting with each other. When a child is engaged in talk with a teacher, there tends to be an asymmetrical pattern of interaction, with the adult taking more responsibility for 'leading' the dialogue (especially in the clarification sequences mentioned above). Consequently the child may be less likely to initiate topics and may generally play a more passive role. Children frequently have available to them many more linguistic resources than we are aware of, but it is easy to overlook this unless we allow them the freedom to take control of the discourse. The teacher's role in assessment is to establish a context for talk and record it, not to direct or control it.

☐ Choose cognitively demanding tasks which are communicative and which the children will enjoy. The children need to have a clear purpose for using language, such as the solving of a problem or reporting back to the class.

☐ Choose tasks which require at least one child to produce *stretches* of language. Situations which require little more than one-word answers do not provide the teacher with much information about children's language abilities.

A tape recorder is a valuable piece of equipment for spoken language assessment, since it allows the teacher to listen to children's language away from the demands of the classroom. (The first use of a tape recorder in the classroom is often accompanied by giggles and whispers, and occasionally by stage fright, but children quickly learn to ignore it!)

Recording the information obtained

There are many ways of recording the information gained from assessment. It can be done informally, particularly if there has been no taping, by keeping anecdotal records as the children are working and talking. (A clipboard is handy for this.) But to be useful for planning future teaching activities, the information needs to be recorded more systematically, so that it can be easily retrieved when it is needed for programming.

Most teachers prefer to adapt or design their own formats, but any format which is to provide the sort of information which will be useful for programming has to take account of the the fact that the concept of language proficiency must include the language *forms* through which the activity or task is carried out. The assessment tasks themselves will focus on the communication of meanings and will involve the child using real language in real contexts, but at the assessment stage the language forms become important. It is after all the forms of language — the grammatical structures and vocabulary — which determine the effectiveness and appropriateness of communication and, in the educational context, largely determine academic success. So while it is important that the assessment tasks involve the production of sustained talk in a purposeful context, the linguistic components need to be separately assessed.

The format shown opposite can be used to record information about a child's performance in a range of communicative situations. The left-hand column of this particular example has been filled in to suit the retelling of a narrative (see pp. 48-50), but the language criteria suited to other situations can readily be substituted beneath the first two points, which will be common to all situations. Beside each point a comment can be written about the child's performance. This allows the assessment to be descriptive, which for the teacher is a far more useful way of gathering information than measuring performance with a mark or a grade. The

ASSESSMENT SHEET: Retelling a narrative (The Terrible Wild Grey Hairy Thing)

Name: Youssef

Date: 20.11.90

1 Ability to carry out the task

Did the child demonstrate the ability to ...	Yes	Yes, but with limited competence (see additional information below)	No demonstration
• understand the task	✓		
• carry out the task	✓		
• include all elements of story	✓	orientation brief: 'once upon a time the lady....'	
• use appropriate vocabulary		✓	
• summarise details		✓ some details summarised; some irrelevant details	
• produce cohesive text by:			
• using range of connectives		used mainly 'and then'	
• having a referent for pronoun		he/she confused, referent for 'it' not clear	
• use direct speech			did not use
• self-correct			no self-correction

2 Additional information on aspects of formal language

Vocabulary/Pronunciation	Fluency	Accuracy
general lack of intonation + expression vocab. O.K. – used some vocab. from text: 'gave him the biggest, fattest sausage of all'	fluent, but speech not always clear – very fast at times	① past tense difficulties: run for ran go for went step for stepped ② pronoun reference: he for she ③ 'start to check the sniff the cat' (unclear)

bottom part of the format relates more specifically to areas of grammar and fluency and allows the teacher to comment on specific strengths or areas of difficulty.

Recording information about each child's language use enables an individual oral language profile to be built up. This is not as massive a task as it appears. It will be simpler and more manageable if, for example, only four or five children are assessed in one week, which will allow each child's spoken language to be assessed four times a year. This is after all a data-gathering exercise, not a test! ESL teachers who work cooperatively with classroom teachers will probably be willing to assist in recording and analysing data too.

Spoken language assessment: a case study

This section is concerned with the analysis of a speaker's language in a particular situation. (A fuller assessment would need to include other aspects of language behaviour, such as confidence and willingness to communicate.) At the time of assessment Youssef, the subject of this case study, was in Year 4. He had arrived in Australia when he was five years old and had entered school speaking minimal English. He spoke Arabic at home, and by Year 4 was fluent in both Arabic and English in the playground.

Youssef's teacher, Bridie, talked of her concern about his English language skills and those of five or six other children in the class. She talked generally about what she saw as their major language difficulties, saying that she felt unsure about the kind of specific help they needed. She had spent a lot of time on her literacy program and she was pleased with the children's involvement in and enjoyment of reading and writing activities, but she now felt that she should pay more attention to the spoken language of the class as a whole.

All the children in the class took part in the retelling assessment described below, which was carried out over a period of three weeks. In addition, Youssef and some of the other children — including those Bridie was most concerned about — were recorded carrying out a barrier game. Bridie felt that it was important to gain a clear idea about the sort of language she should be looking for, and so the barrier game was also used with three of her most competent speakers. Their language provided a good model of what might be expected and, as with the retelling, made it easier to see the areas in which Youssef and other children needed help.

The barrier game 'Find the Difference' (p. 36)

As in all barrier games, Youssef and his partner could not see each other's pictures and information was shared through language. It is this more 'removed' language which places greater linguistic demands on the child, but which is important in encouraging abstract thought and as a bridge into literacy. (In terms of the language continuum described on pp. 31-32, the language that this sort of activity requires would probably fit around Text 2.) The activity required the children to be able to:

Find the Difference

- express position
- ask appropriate questions
- identify clearly the people and things in the picture
- respond to the needs of their partners, either by offering clarification or by responding to a request for clarification.

What was Youssef able to do?

- Youssef understood and completed the task, was able to respond to requests for clarification and to ask for clarification himself.
- He was able to ask yes/no questions.
- He was able to identify the position of objects in the picture.
- He was able to identify the people in the picture.

Where did Youssef need support?

At first sight it seemed as though Youssef had little difficulty in producing the appropriate language to carry out this task. However, when we listened to two native speakers of the same age carrying out the same task, it became evident that there were areas in Youssef's English which lacked precision and fluency.

Although Youssef was able to describe position, he used only four expressions to do so (*in, on, beside, out of*). The two native speakers each used on average twelve expressions. These included *close to, out of, at, under, up, just down from, just below, to the right of, on the left, just across from, just by, over, up, by the, over the top of*. Similarly, in identifying the people Youssef used only minimal description. The native speakers used lengthy nominal groups to identify with precision the people they were referring to (*the boy sitting next to the girl with long hair; one of the children ... the boy who is sitting by the boy with spiky hair*). In addition, Youssef did not always produce context-free language (for example, he referred to *the girl facing this way*) and here the native speakers used more appropriate language (*the girl on the left of, on the right of*).

Like many bilingual children, Youssef had basic coping strategies in English for oral communicative activities such as these, but he appeared not able to produce the finer distinctions of language. Consequently the range of meanings that the more competent speakers had the resources for was beyond him. It is easy to overlook the help that such children need, because they appear to be coping, but as Chapter 2 pointed out, it is these 'gaps' that we must be aware of if children like Youssef are to have the same access to learning as their peers.

Retelling a narrative

Youssef was also recorded retelling a story. He was one of a number of children in the class who had listened to and discussed the same story and were then asked to retell it. To provide a real audience, the children were taped retelling the story to another child who had not heard it. Children could, if they preferred, retell the story on their own, in which case it was suggested to them that the tape could be used with younger children in the school. Once the children were familiar with the story, the retelling was done without reference to the book. (Allowing children to use the book creates a tendency to describe 'what is happening' rather than to retell.) The story chosen was *The Terrible Wild Grey Hairy Thing* by Jean Chapman. The book has great appeal to children of this age, and also has a clear story line.

The task required the children to:

- have an understanding of story structure

- sequence events using appropriate connective words

- express past time

- use vocabulary appropriate to the story to describe characters and what they do

- speak clearly and use appropriate stress and intonation patterns

- be aware of the needs of the audience.

(Since the listeners did not know the story, the speaker had to 'create the context' and not assume any prior knowledge or shared understanding. Using *he* all the way through, for example, can lead to confusion unless the audience knows who *he* refers to.)

Part of Youssef's retelling is included here, and also the retelling of a fluent native speaker, so that some of the omissions or 'gaps' are more easily identified.

> *Youssef:* once upon a time the lady was making some sausages and she made a big fat one and she made a lot for winter ... and for her family ... so she got some of them and she start to hang them up on her wall and the baby accidentally step on the cat and he tickled the lady and she fell down and all the sausages fell all over the place ... and then one fell behind the tool box and the lady start to dust and it got dirty and it became a terrible big monster and there was big smell ... and the lady start to check the sniff the cat and she sniff the baby and she scrubbed and cleaned and smashed the pillows ...

> *Paul:* one day a fat lady was making some sausages ... she was making heaps and heaps of sausages ... she was making so many sausages that they would last her family for a year ... but she was putting them up on nails above her on the ceiling ... and the baby was chasing the cat around at that time ... the cat jumped up and tickled the fat lady's leg ... so she fell down and all the sausages fell on the floor too ... but there was one great big one that got stuck behind a tool box and it stayed there for ages getting mouldy ... one day the fat lady did her spring-cleaning and by that time the big sausage had gone mouldy and was growing whiskers ...

Youssef was able to complete the retelling, but for anyone not already familiar with the story his version would have been very difficult to understand. All parts of the narrative structure (setting, events, complication and resolution) were included, but the text lacked cohesion and was presented as a string of events linked with *and*. (Youssef used *and* twenty-eight times in a little over two minutes of tape.) The lack of alternative ways to connect and sequence ideas produces discourse which seems unstructured. In addition, Youssef used only the simple past tense and made several errors, producing the stem form only on several occasions (e.g. *run* for *ran*, *go* for *went*, *sniff* for *sniffed*).

A comparison with the native speakers made these difficulties more evident. On average their retellings were twice as long. Instead of relying on *and* as the main connective, they used a range of other expressions, particularly those indicating time sequence (e.g. *later, at that time, one day, eventually, a few weeks later, by that time*). They summarised details (note the use of *spring-cleaning* in Paul's retelling). They made a lot of use of direct speech, with appropriate expression and intonation. In addition, all the more competent speakers made many self-corrections as they were speaking. This requires a degree of confidence and language knowledge which Youssef seemed not to have. (The ability to self-correct appears to be an indication of language development in all areas of language.)

The difficulties and omissions in a child's oral language will almost certainly be transferred to literacy activities, where, because of the nature of written text, they immediately become more obvious. Often it is not until mid-primary that such language difficulties become apparent, and then, often, they are seen as being related to ability rather than to language. Recording and analysing Youssef's speech made it possible to identify in detail specific areas of difficulty. It is unlikely that all of these would have been noted if his speech had not been recorded. Of course it would be wrong to jump to conclusions about a child's language needs and abilities on the basis of one recording, but for a class teacher who also has other information about the children in the class, it is a useful tool to indicate the areas in which children need support. For Youssef these can be summarised as:

- identifying and describing people and things with precision
- expressing position accurately and precisely using a range of language items
- expressing a sequence of events using a range of connectives
- expressing past time.

How can this information be translated into the classroom program?

Once information about children has been collected, it needs to be put to good use! The information about Youssef and other children in the class was translated into the class program by becoming a starting point from which Bridie made programming decisions. Since there were other children in the class who had similar language needs, she decided to form skills groups. (Skills groups are also discussed in Chapter 9.) These were not ability groups, and Bridie felt very strongly that the children were not being streamed. Instead the children came together at certain times during the week when

Bridie was able to give them, as a small group, more guidance and teaching time to meet their specific language needs. This organisation was also a way of individualising her classroom program to take into account the specific needs of individuals, while not involving thirty individual programs.

The school in which Bridie works does not have an ESL teacher, but for those schools which do, the formation of skills groups is a useful organisational strategy. The ESL teacher can, for example, work with such groups for a certain part of each day, and this makes good use of specialist skills within the mainstream classroom. Skills groups are *not* a permanent grouping (it would be inappropriate for them to be so, since that would reduce the opportunity for children to hear good language models) and can be disbanded whenever the specific needs are felt to have been met.

To practise and extend the language areas in which Youssef and other children needed support, Bridie devised a number of activities which gave them opportunities both to hear good models of English and to practise using the language themselves. The activities were related to the content of the regular program. For example, the class social studies unit was on caring for the environment, and so the pictures chosen for a 'Find the Difference' barrier game illustrated a creek beside a picnic ground. One picture showed large amounts of rubbish, and the other a clean creek and an abundance of wild life. (This game was very easy to make. Bridie took two photocopies of a line drawing of a creek and picnic area and added rubbish to one and wildlife to the other. Then she photocopied both pictures again.)

During the term Youssef's group and other children in the class took part in a number of activities related to their particular needs, including the following.

The barrier game (described above). This was always played with a competent English speaker so that less competent speakers had good language models. The game allowed the children to hear and practise positional language and the descriptive language associated with identifying people and things. It proved very popular, and during craft time one afternoon Bridie took up an offer made by two of her best artists to produce a similar game!

An information-transfer activity. The children drew a picture based on a written description. This provided models of positional and descriptive language and also used the environmental theme.

A sequencing activity. Youssef sequenced a set of picture cards to retell a story. He first retold this orally and then as a written piece.

A retelling activity. The children, as part of their regular literature activities, were used to producing story maps from narrative texts. In this activity they used maps to retell a story onto tape. The maps provided them with support for their retelling, while not detracting from the value of the retelling itself. This time they were given an opportunity to listen to the tape and rerecord it if they wished. A number of the children (including Youssef) were keen to rerecord once they had heard their first version. The process of listening to their own retelling, discussing how it could be improved and then rerecording proved to be a very useful learning strategy, and one which has continued in this class. Some of these tapes are used with infant children in the school for a variety of purposes.

A text-matching activity. This involved matching diagrams and text in the description of a process — how acid rain is formed — and provided models of the language associated with sequencing.

Some practical considerations

Time is always at a premium. How do you find time to make games, analyse language and organise a variety of classroom activities to meet a range of needs, as well as 'teach'? Part of the answer is not to attempt to do it all at once! The games suggested are made as they are needed and over time will build up to a useful personal resource collection. Often other teachers can share them, and some parents are willing to assist with the production of resources.

The comments Bridie made at the end of term also illuminate some practical aspects of the developments in her assessment and programming.

'I found that assessing only a few children at a time made it manageable. What I feel pleased about now is the fact that I really do feel I am meeting the children's needs. I feel differently about assessment and see it as necessary for making decisions about my program. Having this information about the children made programming easier because I knew what I wanted to achieve.

'At the beginning I was worried that there wasn't time to do a lot of extra language work. I was worried also that the children who were doing any special activities would be missing out on something else. Then I started to see the language as part of my program rather than something extra, as a *part* of the content I was teaching.'

The learning situations, activities and games described in this chapter and the previous one have a specific language focus and are designed to meet particular language needs. For children learning English as a second language they provide essential language support in a context of planned intervention. Including activities which focus on the language of planned content is essential for children who are learning in their second language. However, less focused activities are also important in providing support for language development, and a good whole language program should provide many other opportunities for children to hear and use spoken language for a variety of purposes.

CHAPTER FIVE

Integrating New Arrival Children in the Classroom

The term 'new arrival' refers to those children who are newly arrived in Australia. If they have come from a country where English is taught at school, they may speak, or read and write, some English, but for many it will be their first experience of the language. When a new arrival comes into your class, it may seem as if he or she can do nothing at all and will be unable to take part in any normal classroom activities. But remember that these children have already acquired one language, have developed many concepts in that language and may be literate in it as well. It is important that you remain positive towards them and their language, and that at every opportunity you display confidence in their ability to learn English and advance in learning.

This chapter contains suggestions and strategies to help this to occur. Classroom strategies to support newly arrived children should aim to:

- make the learner feel secure and comfortable
- allow the learner to participate and interact
- help the learner to achieve.

Before the child arrives ...

☐ Sometimes you may know in advance that a new arrival will be joining your class. After checking that the placement is appropriate to the child's age, take the opportunity to talk to your class about the new student and discuss with them how they might be able to help. Shaping positive attitudes towards the new arrival is important because this will be an important factor in the progress he or she will make in English. Many classes are used to children arriving with no English, but if this will be a new experience for your class, point out some of the difficulties the child may have, such as being unable to talk to anyone and so finding it hard to join in playground games and make friends. Emphasise the fact that he or she is able to speak another language. Some of the children may be happy to volunteer to look after the new arrival when he or she first arrives. A class which has some understanding of the language learning task being faced by newly arrived children can usually contribute many ideas as to how they can be helped, and will often develop a sense of pride in their growing achievements.

☐ Encourage the child's family, if it is possible, to keep the child at home for at least a few days after arriving in Australia to become oriented to new surroundings and neighbourhood, and in some cases to recover from the effects of long journeys and jet lag. At this time a few days spent with the family at home will probably be of more benefit than a few extra days spent at school.

☐ Find out as much as you are able about the new arrival. Information should include the languages spoken and previous schooling. In some cases children will have had uninterrupted schooling and be fully literate in their mother tongue. At the other extreme are children whose schooling has been severely interrupted or perhaps non-existent. Children's previous experiences will shape their expectations of their new school, and an understanding of their background is very important in helping to provide an optimal learning environment.

☐ Find out and teach your class how to say 'hello' in the child's language.

☐ Try to locate adults or children within the school community who speak the same language.

When the child arrives ... the first few days

☐ If you are able to arrange it, an hour alone with the new arrival when he or she first arrives will help you get to know each other. It is you with whom the child will spend most time at school, not the ESL teacher or other support staff, and so it is important that you begin to develop a relationship with each other as soon as possible. Take the time to show the child around the school, so that he or she will know where places like the toilets, tuckshop and library are. Talk to the child as normally as possible even if there seems to be no response — and resist the urge to say things louder if you appear not to be understood!

☐ Establish a buddy system. If possible, choose children who speak the same language as well as others who will provide good English models. Be sensitive to the fact that some children who have learned English may not want to use their first language with the new child. Do not try to force language choice, but remember that your own positive attitude towards a child's first language is important. While the buddy system should allow the new arrival to hear good English, it is probably more important in the early stages to choose children who are friendly and talkative, rather than selecting only on the basis of competence in English.

☐ Use an interpreter or another child to make sure the new arrival knows and understands regular classroom routines, such as going to the toilet or what happens at recess and lunch.

☐ Teach some basic survival language. It can be quite traumatic for children to be unable to ask to go to the toilet or to say they feel sick!

☐ Discover how much English the new arrival has. Ask simple questions first, such as: *What's your name? How old are you?* See if the child can identify in English things like parts of the body, clothes and classroom objects. Find out if the child can count in English, recognise numerals and can follow simple classroom instructions such as: *Sit down, Stand up* or *Come here.* If any of these cause difficulty, stop before the child becomes demoralised or confused, and affirm any responses which the child makes in the mother tongue.

☐ Allow the new arrival the right to remain silent. It may be weeks or longer before he or she has the confidence to say anything in English. Listening and watching how other people are behaving and responding is an important part of learning another language, and the child is working hard at making sense of what at first will seem a meaningless jumble of sound. Before the child begins to speak, watch for signs of comprehension, such as the following of instructions. Look also at how comfortable he or she seems to be in interacting with other children. Very reserved, shy children often take much longer to begin to speak in English. Watching and listening time allows children to scan and absorb routines before being expected to participate fully themselves.

☐ Try to become aware of non-verbal cues that you may be using yourself and make these clear to the child. Many misunderstandings occur because of cultural differences. For example, it may not be respectful in the child's culture for a student to maintain direct eye contact with a teacher, or the child may be unaware of what is the normal personal space for Australians and feel that you are behaving inappropriately when you stand close or bend down to speak.

Providing support in the classroom

☐ At times let pairs of children develop and teach mini 'lessons' to the new arrival, such as teaching how to tell the time. This can be just as beneficial for the 'teachers' as for the learner.

☐ Create opportunities for the new arrival to participate in classroom situations which do not require language. He or she should take part in all the routines and rituals of the classroom and have access to the full range of activities and equipment available for all children. Even before they have developed any English, it is important that children are *involved* and feel part of the class. Games like 'Statues' or 'Dead Lions'; activities such as dressing up, playing with sand, dancing or mime; curriculum areas such as art, craft, music or sport — all provide opportunities for involvement.

☐ Build up a scrapbook. The child can cut up magazines and label sets of objects with the help of a classmate. The pictures can often be related to the vocabulary of specific topics that the class is studying.

☐ Involve the new arrival in lots of opportunities to listen to English and interact with peers in a small group. The peer group is a major resource for language learning, and a wish to communicate with one's peers is a strong motivation for using and learning language. When the child starts to speak English, it is also far less threatening to do so in a small group than in front of a whole class.

☐ Use picture talks. This provides visual support for the language the learner is hearing.

☐ Provide activities which use skills that require understanding rather than the productive skills of speaking or writing. For example, choose activities that have a concrete focus and require manipulation of some sort.

☐ Provide a variety of activities where the child can work with others in less structured situations. A maths area, a hobby display area, a science and nature table, a painting area, a shop or a dressing-up area are all good language learning environments, which are equally suitable for younger and older grades.

☐ Organise other adults, such as parents, to take the new arrival with other members of the class around the neighbourhood to visit the library, shopping centre, police station or post office. Record the experience through drawings, audio tape or photographs.

☐ Recall events orally, especially excursions in which the new arrival has taken part, using drawings, photographs, objects collected or tapes. Encourage everyone to contribute items. Use these to develop a written record through wall stories, overheads, charts or captioned photographs.

☐ Use 'written conversations'. The child begins by writing briefly about anything he or she wishes and the teacher writes a response, where possible using this to model the correct forms of any words or structures which have been used incorrectly. The child responds in turn (and, in the example shown opposite, it is worth noting how the child's responses follow the teacher's modelling — e.g. the use of the word *mountains* or the structure *they have snow*). The writing can continue over several days, or for as long as interest in the topic is sustained. Used daily, it is an excellent way to lead the learner gradually into the patterns of written English.

☐ Continue to encourage the use of the first language with peers where this is possible, particularly for explanations and in problem-solving situations.

climbing

Did you mountain climb in Korea?

Who went with you? mum and dad and jame yes

Did you get scared? NO

Are the mountains very high? NO
the mountaine is Are No't.

Do they always have snow on them? No

What months do they have snow?

they have snow in disember

Ben entered Year 5 with almost no English. This written conversation with his teacher took place about two months later.

☐ Give instructions clearly and precisely.

☐ Use open-ended questions so that the child is able to respond at his or her own level.

☐ Use visual aids such as diagrams, maps, videos, pictures or mime to help make meaning clear.

☐ Try to get information from the learner rather than always presenting it.

☐ Provide activities where the language is predictable or repetitive. Many books are based upon the repetition of a particular structure or event. Rhymes and songs are often repetitive and will also help develop the rhythms and stress of spoken English.

☐ Include some activities which recycle newly learned language.

☐ As far as possible design activities which *either* use known language patterns to teach new vocabulary, *or* use known vocabulary to model new language patterns.

☐ Use activities which involve real communication and where the emphasis is on meaning (such as the barrier games described in Chapter 3).

☐ Use whole class activities where the new arrival can join in as much as he or she feels able. Being part of a large group and reading aloud from a big book, or reciting poems or singing allows the learner to practise the language in a supportive and non-threatening environment.

☐ In the early stages choose books and print materials not only in terms of their language difficulty but also in terms of their cultural content. Stories about camping, barbecues, days at the beach or other aspects of Australian culture will initally be quite alien to some children.

☐ Where appropriate, give the new arrival opportunities to continue learning in familiar ways. Some children will have been used to large amounts of rote learning and will be very successful at this. When the child first arrives, you may need to be flexible in your teaching methods and be prepared to compromise in some things! Some children may also be unused to group work, or to discovery-type learning, and at times will enjoy working quietly alone. Gradually encourage the child into the ways of learning that normally occur in your classroom.

Building on literacy skills

If the new arrival can read and write in the mother tongue, this will greatly facilitate the development of literacy in English. The following strategies are useful for children who are already literate.

☐ Allow the child to write in the first language. Sometimes it will be possible to find an adult, such as a parent, who will conference with the child and perhaps translate the writing into English. It is possible in this way to build up a bilingual book from the child's writing. If the mother tongue and English translation are on facing pages, the child will have an excellent model of a whole text in English which is also understandable. Even when no one is available to translate or conference, allowing the new arrival to write in the mother tongue is still valuable because it gives the child an opportunity to show what he or she is able to do, and to be involved in the same activity as the rest of the class. However, allow choice of language for writing activities and do not insist on a child writing in his or her first language; some children are unwilling to do so and prefer to make immediate attempts in English.

☐ Encourage the new arrival to continue to read regularly in the mother tongue. Your school or local library may have some books in the child's language. Try to get advice about choice of books, especially about appropriateness for the age level and the type of language (it may be in a different dialect to the one the new arrival speaks).

☐ Provide a bilingual dictionary or encourage the child to obtain one. Make sure that it provides a two-way translation — for example, Chinese to English and English to Chinese. Using a dictionary helps the child to become independent and makes use of existing skills.

Getting settled

Many newly arrived children settle into school quite happily and cope well with the task of learning a new language. Usually children who have migrated will have had time to get used to the idea of moving to a new country, and it will probably have been discussed and planned for long before they arrive. Many families will already have contacts in the new country and a good idea of what they are coming to. They may be joining friends and relatives already living in Australia and have the support of a strong ethnic community. Some children will already have other members of their family at the same school.

However, even normally happy and confident children can become frustrated or angry in a situation where they cannot make other people understand them, or which they cannot understand themselves. After having been competent language users and learners in their home country, children suddenly find themselves not understanding even simple tasks and instructions. Listening to and trying to concentrate on a new language is also very tiring, even for adults and even for a short time. Such concentration hour after hour, and day after day, can make children very tired.

Other factors may also interfere with learning. Many newly arrived children will be missing the friends and relatives left behind, their home, and all the known routines that have been part of their lives until now. Their families may have few networks of support and may also be experiencing emotional or financial difficulty, and initially perhaps even regretting the move to Australia. The child may find the new school very different from any he or she has known before, and may be expected to learn in totally new ways.

The difficulties associated with migration can be much more extreme in the case of refugees. Refugees have not willingly left their homeland. They have left for a variety of reasons, sometimes because of political upheaval, sometimes as a result of war. A common response to the question *Why did you leave?* is *To find freedom.* Some refugees may not have chosen the country they have come to. They may have been told, while in a refugee camp, where their future home was to be. They have usually come with the minimum of belongings and few, if any, tangible reminders of home, such as photographs or other mementos. Or, as one adult refugee said, 'I don't have anything here that links me to my past.'

Migration, even when planned, is a great upheaval; it can be a traumatic experience for adults and is often described as a grieving experience. Children have even less control over the new environment and experience. Sometimes their frustration and deep unhappiness will result in difficult classroom behaviour, and a few children become aggressive and disruptive, constantly restless, tearful or very withdrawn.

It is important to be aware that disruptive and disturbing behaviour may be caused by what the child is experiencing and is not necessarily indicative of his or her usual behaviour. Of course a newly arrived child should be expected to observe the same classroom rules and behaviour as the rest of the class, and as far as possible follow normal classroom routines. Teachers themselves can do little about many of the stresses on newly arrived families, but it is vital that in the classroom the child feels accepted and is given many opportunities to be successful, however small they may be. It is also important that good communication is set up with parents, and ideas about how to go about this are included in the final chapter of this book. The ideas below are aimed at ensuring success and building up confidence.

☐ Allow the child many opportunities to do what he or she is best at. A child who is good at craft activities, for example, can be allowed to spend extra time on them. Where appropriate, alert specialist teachers so that they spend an extra five minutes with the child during the class.

☐ Pace the activities during the day so that the child does not become exhausted. Activities which do not require the new arrival to produce language, such as listening to taped stories, should be interspersed with activities which require speaking and writing. Allow the child some quiet time during the day when he or she is free to choose what to do and can 'switch off' from the demands of the classroom.

☐ Set up situations where the new arrival is the expert. Once newly arrived children have some English, encourage them, if they are happy to do so, to talk to a group of children about their own experiences and culture, or demonstrate specific skills, or teach a poem or read a story in their own language.

☐ Praise all success and share all achievements with the child's parents.

☐ Remember that responding to what a learner is *trying* to say is more important at this stage than how he or she is saying it. Correct gently by accepting, expanding or completing partially correct or incomplete utterances. Do not do it at a time when it interrupts the normal flow of communication, and be prepared to wait a little longer for a response than you would normally do.

☐ Give the new arrival opportunities to hear and practise social language, such as asking for something, asking someone to do something, saying thank you and expressing disagreement politely. It is easy to make the assumption that a child is being rude and aggressive when it may be the case that the appropriate language for a situation has not yet been learned.

☐ Make the child feel a useful member of the class. He or she should be expected to perform most of the classroom jobs that other children do, such as giving out paper, collecting rubbish and general tidying and cleaning jobs. He or she can also accompany children taking messages to other classes or teachers.

— CHAPTER SIX —

The Mother Tongue in the Classroom

Why use the mother tongue?

The use of the mother tongue in the classroom can be a tremendous support for children learning English as a second language, particularly for those in the beginning years of school. Most kindergarten children who enter school with little or no English are, by necessity, expected to learn within the confines of a very limited range of language — their current level of development in English. These children have full capacity for learning, but in an English-only class they are without the language which will allow them to do so. In this situation their cognitive and conceptual development may be slowed down or hampered while they are acquiring sufficient fluency in English.

There are many reasons that can be given for the use of the mother tongue in school, but there are three that are of special significance.

1 Using the mother tongue for learning allows children to draw on their *total* language experience and so continue their conceptual development. The use of the mother tongue in the teaching of basic concepts not only facilitates this development, but also makes it easier for the child to understand, and therefore to learn, the *English* related to these concepts. In addition, where children can draw on all their skills, the teacher can evaluate their learning more thoroughly.

2 The mother tongue helps to provide a social-emotional environment in which the basic conditions for learning can occur. It provides a link to the language of

the home and family, helping to lessen the trauma and alienation children may experience in a new environment, surrounded by an unknown language. The use of the first language does much to maintain confidence and self-esteem because it is a signal that the classroom *includes* the child. It says: 'We accept your language and — by implication — your family, your ethnicity and your culture.'

3 It is sound educational practice to build on a learner's competencies and abilities. Ignoring children's first languages is wasteful because it ignores one of the greatest resources they bring to school.

The first years of schooling are critical in the development of confidence and self-esteem, and in building up the patterns of learning that will continue through school. A cycle of failure and low self-esteem started at this time becomes increasingly hard to break as the child moves through school. Children beginning school with no English are particularly at risk of being caught in this cycle. They may find that by the time they have learned sufficient English to begin learning in it, most other people in the class have learned to read; even by the end of the first year at school they may be 'learning to fail'. Early intervention provided through mother tongue support, as well as English, allows children to be successful learners.

There are many ways in which the mother tongue can be used in the classroom, ranging from a full K-6 bilingual program to occasional mother tongue support in class by a bilingual teacher's aide or parent.

Bilingual programs

Ideally a bilingual program operates through the school from K-6. It involves part of the curriculum being taught through the medium of the mother tongue, and aims at developing cognitive and literacy skills in both the first language and in English.

In many parts of the world speaking two or more languages is a part of life, and current estimates suggest that there are more bilinguals than monolinguals world wide. A language conscious nation should see bilingualism as an asset, and ideally our schools would be resourced to respond to their multilingual populations and be able to educate all children — including monolingual English speakers — to become proficient and confident in two languages. Opportunities for bilingual education would help to reverse the current situation, where vast amounts of our potential linguistic resources remain neglected and untapped in our schools.

In reality, and frequently because of funding-related issues, many bilingual programs are 'transitional', meaning that mother tongue support is gradually withdrawn as the child learns to cope in English. Although such programs do not aim at the ultimate maintenance of the mother tongue, they nevertheless remain a very important option for schools which have large numbers of second language speakers who share the same mother tongue. A well-organised and well-planned transitional bilingual program offers many children perhaps the best chance they

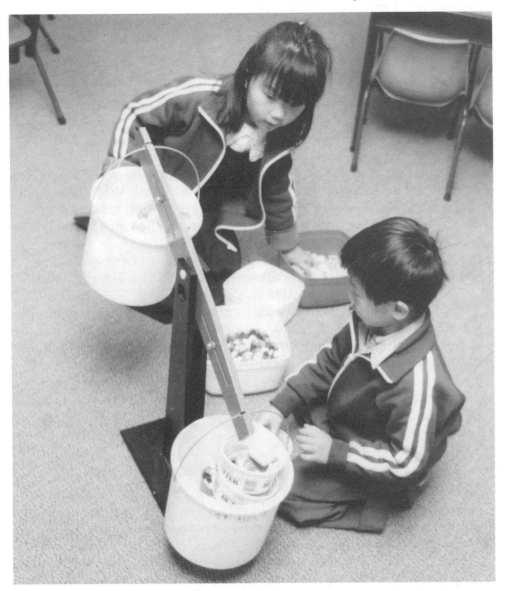

Learning something is easier if you can use your first language — in this case, Cantonese.

have to develop English, increase their capacity for learning and maintain self-concept.

These programs normally operate only in the first two to three years of schooling. Their main aim is to support conceptual development through the use of the mother tongue. There are many organisational options for such a program, and choice will depend on the numbers of children involved, the availability of teachers, and the many other curriculum demands that are part of a school. Whatever the choice of organisation, there are two key elements in any bilingual approach.

1 The children's *first language* (Arabic, Spanish, Vietnamese, etc.) is used to teach some areas of the curriculum, such as maths, social studies or science.

2 The children are also exposed to a source of *English* language models related to the same content area and concepts.

Both these elements are essential to a bilingual program. In other words, the children are not only learning through the use of the mother tongue, but *also* have opportunities to develop English.

Each language is used without translation, and the two languages are kept *separate* as far as possible (for example, by their separated use in the timetable), so that the children are involved in extended stretches of both languages. Videos of Spanish bilingual classes where the bilingual teacher simply provided on-the-spot translations as the class teacher was speaking illustrate the potential disadvantage of approaches where the languages are not kept separate (Wong-Filmore 1982). The children's attention tended to wander when they heard English; they 'switched off' because they had learned to wait for the Spanish translation. Similarly the English speaking teacher — probably quite unconsciously — used less English with the children and made fewer attempts at making her language comprehensible, presumably because she also knew that what she said would be translated! The children were therefore limited in their opportunity to develop English, and Spanish was not being used for long enough stretches for there to be sufficient conceptual development. There will be times where an instant translation is all that is required to clarify a particular issue or classroom instruction for a child, but bilingual approaches should not depend on this as an organising principle for the program.

One school's approach to a transitional program

This school's program operates in the first three years. The organisation of the kindergarten (the first year of school) is described here, but other year levels follow a similar pattern, with a gradual decrease in the amount of Spanish used.

The school has two kindergarten classes. Seven children in one class, and eleven in the other, speak Spanish as their first language and little or no English. Seventy per cent of all kinder children are from language backgrounds other than English.

The eighteen Spanish speaking children come together with a Spanish speaking teacher for about two hours at the start of each day. During this period they follow the class program, which at this time is maths, social studies and science, but they are taught through the medium of Spanish. At this time the other kinder children are engaged in the same activities in English.

For the remainder of the day the Spanish speaking children return to their own classes and operate in English. At planned times during the week their class teachers, with support from the ESL teacher, consolidate with the whole class the maths and science work that has been covered, and at this time the Spanish speaking children have an opportunity to hear and use the specific English language structures related to the concepts they have been developing in Spanish.

There are several issues related to programs like this, and it may take some time before all the teachers involved feel convinced of the value of the program. In the school described the teachers had many questions when the program started. Some are included here, together with the answers they now give.

Will the children be missing out when they leave the classroom?

'No, they are continuing to learn the same things as everybody else; they are simply doing it in a different language.'

Will their English suffer?

'No, as long as they are given sufficient opportunity to hear and use the English associated with the learning. We now find that they develop English much more quickly than the children who have not done the "learning" first in their own language.'

We try not to 'withdraw' children. Is the bilingual program another 'withdrawal' program?

'No, because the bilingual program is not isolated from the class program. The children leave the class because that is easier than having two teachers in one classroom space speaking different languages! The classroom program remains the focus for all of us — both class teachers, the Spanish teacher and the ESL teacher. We plan it together.'

What about the children who are second language learners but who are not Spanish speaking? Do you feel they are missing out?

'We would like to offer the same opportunities for all children to learn in their mother tongue, but like most other schools we do not have enough resources to do this. So we have chosen to support at least some of the children — the largest group — in their mother tongue. But the bilingual program has had positive spin-offs for the other children too. Because we have an extra teacher during bilingual program time, we are working with smaller groups and can give more individual support to the other children. Also there is more acceptance now of other languages in the school by the teachers and children.' (See the section below: *Other ways to support the mother tongue.*)

How do you feel the children have benefited through the program?

'Children are understanding concepts in English much more quickly.'

'I have noticed a great increase in the self-esteem and confidence of these children.'

'The children are no longer falling behind in the home class, because they are continuing to learn in Spanish.'

'I now know whether a child has a problem with the language (English), or whether there is a problem with the understanding of the concept itself.'

'Parents are much more confident in communicating with the school.'

'Parents now see their language as of value.'

Cardenas (1986, p. 47), writing about the role of the mother tongue in education, refers to the analogy made by Bruce Gaarder, a long-time advocate of bilingual education in the United States. In developing a rationale for bilingual education, Gaarder compares the use of language to a window through which a child interacts with the environment, thereby gaining the experiences which produce learning. He suggests that the window of the minority language child is blue, while the window of the English speaking child is rose-coloured. On entering an English-only school, the child who is used to looking through a blue window is told: 'From now on you must learn to use the rose window for interacting with your environment.' Then the blue window is covered and the child is left staring at a blank wall instead. Should the child say, 'I don't see any rose window,' the school will reply: 'That's because we haven't built it yet, but if you keep looking at the blank wall, we will eventually put a pink window there.' Cardenas points out that staring at a blank wall does little to facilitate learning! The value of a bilingual program is that it allows the child to go on learning, and increases the capacity for learning, while the rose window is being built.

In-class support

Support can also be given by a bilingual aide or teacher within the class while the regular classroom activities are going on. The same principles should still operate.

- The children must have extended time to take part in the same learning activities as other children, but in their first language.

- The children must have access to English through peer group work and teacher models.

- The bilingual adult should use the child's first language as consistently as possible. The dominant language (English) exerts a natural 'pull', and bilingual adults working in this way need to be aware of this and resist the temptation to slip into English.

Working with a bilingual helper

Bilingual helpers, whether they are teachers' aides or parents, have a rich experience of language and culture and an understanding and knowledge of their own ethnic group in the Australian setting. Although they may be involved with any children in the class, they will be of special help to those children whose language they speak. They may be able to help interpret students' problems, explain aspects of student behaviour and give teachers some indication as to why children may not be learning. They are able to liaise with parents and alert teachers to potential areas of cultural misunderstanding or difficulty within a particular unit of work. They may also be willing to assist in various cultural activities. They are valuable people, and if you are working with bilingual helpers, their unique knowledge and language skills should not be wasted.

They are usually not trained teachers, or they may have been trained overseas and be accustomed to very different classroom practices and methodologies. To help the bilingual helper to work as effectively as possible with you and ensure the maximum benefit for the children, it is important that you both know what each of you expects. The suggestions below are intended to help establish a good working relationship and develop a way of working which will be most beneficial to the children.

☐ Get to know the bilingual helper well, particularly his or her interests and skills. Aim to develop a positive, trusting relationship.

☐ Consider how the helper appears before the children and the parents. He or she should be seen as a colleague.

☐ Establish clear discipline practices early on — what to say, what to do and who is responsible.

☐ Make sure the helper understands the specific tasks in which he or she will be involved. It is important that the helper is clear about what the children will be doing, what the purpose of the activity is and what part he or she will be playing.

☐ Make sure that you are making use of the bilingual skills and other personal skills of the helper. Involve him or her in program planning, or plan for the helper's involvement within the classroom.

The responsibility for the class always remains with the teacher, but a well-supported bilingual helper can be of great assistance to you and a great support for the children.

Some other ways to support the mother tongue

Even without a bilingual program or the regular assistance of a bilingual helper, it is still possible for a teacher to reflect the children's mother tongue within the classroom. Language and cultural diversity is not something that should be confined to a single group of children or one slot in the timetable. It should permeate the classroom and everything that occurs within it. The following ideas can serve as a starting point.

☐ Build mother tongue stories into the program, using tapes at listening posts or making available books in the mother tongue. Older children or parents may help produce tapes.

☐ Invite parents, grandparents or other members of the ethnic community to read or tell stories, sometimes to the whole class. A story could be told in the mother tongue and then retold in English. The experience of hearing another

Developing skills in two languages: reading and writing Arabic is part of this school's curriculum.

language and learning that this is also a way of communicating is valuable for English monolingual children too. Be sensitive to the fact that not all parents will be literate in their first language, but they may often have great storytelling talents.

☐ Display the children's mother tongues in the classroom. Label objects around the classroom and display the children's writing.

☐ Build up a stock of bilingual books based on the children's own writing. Children who are literate in their mother tongue, or parents, may help with translation. If the English and the mother tongue are on facing pages, all children will have access to the text.

☐ Encourage bilingual children to write their names in their mother tongue, and perhaps the names of other children in the class too.

☐ Incorporate song and related dance or drama into the program. A story could be dramatised and presented in English and in the mother tongue at a school assembly.

☐ Use puppets or magnet board figures for children to dramatise in their mother tongue a story that the class has heard in English.

☐ Invite children to teach you and the class a little of their language, such as a song, a greeting, colours or how to count. Each morning for a week say 'good morning' to the class in one of the class languages, and encourage all children to reply.

☐ Use multilingual signs around the school to label places like the school office, the Principal's office, the library and the tuckshop. Put up welcome signs in the languages of the school.

☐ Provide interpreters at parent-teacher interviews if you feel they are needed (but not the children themselves).

☐ Send school notes home in English and in the mother tongue. Often parents will be happy to assist with translation. Do not be put off by the comment, 'The parents can't read their own language.' There will always be someone in the community who will be able to help them, and it is the message from the school that minority parents are *included* which is important.

☐ Explore cultural diversity within classroom themes. Within topics such as *Me, Our Neighbourhood* or *Food*, children can be encouraged to share their own experiences of culture and language. Try to stress also the commonality between groups: for example, the fact that good nutrition is important to everybody, but that there are different ways of meeting this need.

☐ ABOVE ALL — give a clear indication to parents that the use of their own language with their children will assist their children's learning and will not hinder their development in English. The choice of language which parents use with their children is ultimately a personal one, but parents who feel more confident in their own language, and would prefer to use it with their children, should be reassured of its importance and value.

Our aim in schools should always be to extend a child's range of options and choices. For bilingual children this means that we must foster an environment where they are able to make links and contacts across communities. A second language and culture is not learned by destroying the first. By ignoring the mother tongue, we run the risk of slowing down children's learning and encouraging, often unintentionally, the beginning of a one-way journey away from their families.

CHAPTER SEVEN

Reading in a Second Language

What is reading?

Reading is the process of getting meaning from print. It is not a passive, receptive activity, but requires the reader to be active and thinking. A competent reader reconstructs a writer's message. This reconstruction of meaning is an interactive process between the reader and the text, because the reader also makes a contribution. To get meaning from a text, readers bring their own background knowledge of the 'field', or topic, and their understanding of the language system itself. Without these a piece of text is meaningless to a reader — for example, if it is in an unfamiliar language or about unfamiliar things. To illustrate this, here is a short 'comprehension' exercise.

Read the following text and then answer the questions in complete sentences.

A krinklejup was parling a tristlebin. A barjam stipped. The barjam grupped 'Minto' to the krinklejup. The krinklejup zisked zoelly.

What was the krinklejup doing?

What stipped?

What did the barjam grup?

How did the krinklejup zisk?

Now consider — is this reading? It could be argued that it is, since by using our knowledge about how such language works (and also how traditional comprehension exercises work), we are able to come up with the 'right' answers. Yet we can construct little meaning from this text. We have no clear idea of the writer's intent. Of course, as you were reading, you may have provided the unknown words with a visual image — perhaps you conjured up a mental picture of a krinklejup! If we 'translate' or provide mental pictures for the unfamiliar words, we might begin to build up an idea for ourselves of what this text could be about, but because we have no shared understandings for the meanings of the words, it will be very different from any other reader's interpretation. In only a minimal sense, then, can this be considered reading.

To the same question — is this reading? — a Year 4 child (and a fluent reader) gave an interesting and perceptive response: 'Yes, because I could work out the answers.' Then he added, 'But it's not really reading, because I just went from here,' indicating the questions, 'to here,' indicating the text. 'It didn't go through my head.'

True reading 'goes through your head'. Comprehension is what occurs *during* the reading process. Traditional comprehension questions do not test a reader's comprehension — they test the reader's memory of what *was* comprehended (and of course ability to do the 'comprehension' activity). There is a place for such activities, particularly where the questions are more open-ended and require the reader to make inferences, predict consequences or relate the text in some way to personal experience. But answering questions which relate to the text is 'after the event'. Helping children to develop the skills of reading, on the other hand, means intervening *during* the reading process. This chapter will look at how this process works, where it might break down for children who are reading in their second language, and what intervention strategies may be useful.

What does a fluent reader do?

Many models of reading have been put forward during the last thirty years. Some suggest that reading is a 'bottom up' process, where the reader processes print from letter, to word, to sentence, to whole text. 'Bottom up' theories led to reading schemes which focused heavily on phonics and isolated sight words in the initial stages of reading. Other models suggest that reading is a 'top down' process, where the reader's world knowledge and understanding of the topic play a major part in comprehension. All models agree, however, that reading is *active* and involves *a reasoning process*. The model of reading which is now widely accepted is that proposed by Goodman (1967). He suggests that reading is an interactive process involving a transaction between the text and the reader. A fluent reader predicts what he or she is about to read, and then confirms or rejects this prediction on the basis of what follows. Prediction is made on the basis of three systems: semantic, syntactic and graphophonic. These are usually referred to as the 'cueing systems'.

The semantic system

When writers write, any text they produce will be embedded within the framework of their own particular culture and knowledge of the world. If readers do not share this framework, or at least have some understanding of it, they will not be able to fully comprehend the text. We do not have a semantic system available to us to read the text above successfully, because we do not recognise krinklejups and tristlebins or what they are doing (even though we can recode the sounds of the words). Being able to draw on the semantic system means having the world knowledge and cultural knowledge which is relevant to a particular text. Much of what needs to be understood in order to make sense of a text is not actually in the text itself. A reader's existing knowledge framework, or 'schema', is an important factor in helping to reconstruct meaning from text, and it includes familiarity with the particular type of text, such as whether it is a narrative, a poem or a report. (For a description of schema theory, see Anderson and Pearson 1984, or Carrell and Eisterhold 1983.)

A reader also needs to know something about the 'field', or topic, of the text through personal experience or through other reading. For instance, knowing about the seasons enables us to predict the probable word omitted here:

In summer it is hot, and in winter it is _____.

The semantic system is therefore what readers draw on whenever they make links with previous knowledge, and this existing knowledge plays an important part in the process of interpreting new information.

Within a text much of the semantic information is carried in the *content* words. These are the words which create our mental pictures — the nouns, the adjectives and the verbs. Often these words will be very specific to the field of the text. For example, in a text about kangaroos we are likely to find words such as *marsupial, pouch, jump, herbivore,* etc. General topic knowledge is thus very important in comprehension.

The syntactic system

This describes the language system itself. A competent reader predicts on the basis of what is going to sound or 'feel' right. For a competent speaker of the language this is an intuitive process. For example, an English speaker will be able to fill in the gap below (even though it is not an authentic English word) on the basis of knowing many parallel examples in the language.

Mary is a very good shringer. She _____ every day.

Being able to predict that the word will probably be *shrings* depends on knowing (at an intuitive level) three things about how English works:

- the only word that will fit here is one describing what Mary does — a verb

- the verb from *shringer* must be *shring* (generalising from pairs like *writer - write)*

- the word will end in an *s* (generalising from *she writes, she falls,* etc.).

Within the text the syntactic information is carried in the grammatical or *structure* words. These hold the text together and link the content words. Structure words include:

- pronouns (*he, she, it, they, his, her, its, their, him, her, them,* etc.)
- connectives and conjunctions which link ideas (*and, after, before, unless, if, therefore, eventually, although, on the other hand,* etc.)
- auxiliary verbs which join with the main verb (such as *has* in *he has gone;* similarly *had, will be, was, could, might, should,* etc.)
- articles (*a, an, the*)
- word endings (*-ing, -ed, -s,* etc.).

Syntactic information also includes:

- word order (e.g. *fierce, black* and *big* combine to describe *dog* in a particular order: *a big, black, fierce dog,* not *a black, fierce, big dog*)
- word change (e.g. *think* changes to *thought* in the past tense).

The graphophonic system

This is the system for representing the spoken language through written symbols. The sounds of speech are represented by letters and clusters of letters, and punctuation relates to the intonation patterns of spoken language. In the example below, we can predict that the word omitted is likely to be a colour. Without knowing the initial letter and its corresponding sound, we cannot predict the word itself.

It was red, blue and _____.

Given the initial letter *y*, however, we will predict *yellow*.

In the final example, the missing word is *explosion*. It could be predicted on the basis of the semantic information (*explosion, gas* and *destroyed* are related in meaning), the syntactic information (it must be a noun because it follows *the*) and the graphophonic information (it begins with *expl...* and ends with *...n*).

The gas expl_____n destroyed many houses.

Using the three cueing systems

It is clear from these examples that *all three* cueing systems play a part in the reading process. Readers use not one, but three kinds of information simultaneously. Rather than seeing reading as strictly 'top down' or 'bottom up', it is probably more useful for teaching purposes to see reading as a complex process where processing at one level (such as word perception) interacts with processing at another level (such as semantic knowledge). Probably no model can determine what mix of skills and strategies a particular reader employs (and fluent readers will employ different strategies depend-ing on their purpose for reading and their familiarity with the topic of the text). In addition, while effective readers use cueing systems flexibly and in an integrated way, beginning readers are at the stage of trying to 'get it together' and tend to rely more heavily on one or other system. Teachers can only respond to what children are trying to do, build on their existing strategies and help them to develop other strategies that they do not yet have.

The examples above suggest that fluent readers predict and anticipate the text on the basis of semantic and syntactic information, but at the same time use as much of the graphophonic information as they need. They confirm or reject their prediction by asking *does it make sense, does it 'sound' right?* If they confirm that it was correct, they go on reading. If not, they reread the text, this time paying more attention to the print.

For most of the time they are reading, readers will have access to more information than they actually need. Frank Smith (1978) points out that such redundancy provides the reader with great flexibility in the reading process.

But though competent readers, who are using information from all three sources, may have more information than they actually need, we should remember that all models of reading are models of the 'ideal' and are based on what a fluent reader does. This is not necessarily what a six-year-old is able to do, or what a child who is reading in his or her second language might do. Young second language readers are usually *developing* readers with gaps in their cultural and linguistic knowledge of English.

The less competent readers are, the more strategies they need to be able to call on, so that if they are not able to comprehend text using one cueing system, they will be able to call on another. Don Holdaway (1979) writes of putting children in a situation of 'high redundancy': that is, of giving them access to as many sources of information as possible — semantic, syntactic and graphophonic. A balanced reading program will help children to use all three cueing systems.

Where might the process break down for children reading in their second language?

A competent English speaking reader 'samples' the print, picking out key words which carry the most meaning.

A second language learner may not be familiar with the graphophonic symbols and/or not recognise which are the key words carrying the most information.

A competent English speaking reader pre-dicts what is about to be read on the basis of semantic and syntactic information.

A second language learner may not have sufficient background knowledge, cul-tural knowledge or language knowledge to predict, and instead may rely very heavily on graphophonic cues.

A competent English speaking reader tests each prediction.	A second language learner may not be able to tell whether a prediction sounds like English or makes sense.
A competent English speaking reader confirms or rejects each prediction.	A second language learner may be unable to confirm or may wrongly confirm.
A competent English speaking reader corrects when necessary.	A second language learner may not recognise a miscue or may not know how to correct it.

Helping the second language learner — using and extending context

A key factor in the teaching strategies described below is the notion of *extending the context* — broadening the range and knowledge of the cueing systems themselves. All the strategies in some way extend the child's semantic, syntactic and graphophonic knowledge, and focus on the cueing systems *within context*. They are also aimed at helping readers to develop good reading strategies. They are therefore particularly useful for children who are reading in their second language, but they could also be used with English speakers and form part of the regular reading program. Most of the strategies can be adapted for a range of reading levels and types of reading material.

Beginning readers

Shared book

Shared book experiences are an excellent way of introducing second language learners to reading in English. They provide a non-threatening context in which to hear the sounds and patterns of English and relate these to print. Choral reading helps to provide a supportive structure for less confident readers, who can join in as much as they are able in the pressure-free environment of the group.

Reading to children, immersing them in good literature and making it an enjoyable experience facilitates early reading and will greatly affect the attitude that they bring to reading. But simply immersing children in language does not on its own guarantee that they will learn to read. The earlier part of this chapter pointed to the need for children to develop good reading strategies, based on their ability to make use of a variety of contextual clues. The value of shared book as a teaching strategy is dependent on:

- the choice of book in relation to the needs and understandings of the children

- how a teacher uses it.

Choosing books

For second language learners who are also beginning readers, it is important that books are chosen with the following criteria in mind.

☐   The language should sound authentic and be a good model of language in use. Language is likely to be distorted and actually be *more* difficult for second language learners to understand if the choice of words has been governed mainly by an attempt to teach particular phonic skills or use only short, 'simple' words.

☐   Choose books whose topic and setting can be related to the child's own experiences. At some point 'learning to read' becomes 'reading to learn', and reading provides an avenue for discovering new information and ways of thinking. Beginning readers, however, need to be able to make as many links as possible with their own experiences. For this reason books need to be chosen not only for their language but also for their cultural content. Content which is quite alien to children, or has a different connotation for them, will be much more difficult to understand. Refugee children who have encountered real pirates will not bring to a pirate story the same associations of adventure, excitement and fun that the topic may evoke in the minds of Anglo-Celtic children.

☐   Choose books where there are large clear pictures which support the text. Picture clues play an important part in learning to read, and predicting text on the basis of the illustrations is a valuable early reading strategy.

☐   Choose books where the text is repetitive or predictable. Stories which have a simple repetitive chorus, like *The Gingerbread Man*, or a cumulative story line, like *The Elephant and the Bad Baby* or *The Hungry Caterpillar*, encourage children to join in the reading. Hearing and reading the same thing for a second or third time within the same story allows time for comprehension and helps children see themselves as readers.

☐   Choose books which have a clear story line that will serve as a model for children's own narrative writing.

☐   Choose books where the print is clear.

☐   Include books with no text and use them to develop children's own writing.

☐   Choose books which have the potential to be used for:

- innovating on text
- drama
- art and craft activities
- puppet shows
- the sorts of language activities described in the following pages.

Using shared book

☐ Exploit the pictures! Talk about them, ask questions about them. Ask children what they think the story might be about. Encourage them to talk about what they can see in the illustrations. This will help you to see what vocabulary might not be known. Model language that the children appear to have difficulty with. Ask direct questions like 'What is this boy eating?', and also more open-ended questions such as 'What do you like to eat? What do you eat at home?' Open-ended questions which relate what is about to be read to the children's own experiences will help them to extend the context in which the book is being read.

☐ Read a book many times and encourage the children to join in as you are reading. Use a pointer to indicate the words so that you focus the children's attention on the print. Initially read for enjoyment rather than to develop a teaching point. Don't assume that children will grow tired of a story after only a couple of readings. They will enjoy favourite stories being read and reread, and this will also give second language learners more opportunities to comprehend the text.

☐ When the children begin to be able to join in the reading, use a frame to focus first on single sentences, then on words and then on letters (see example overleaf).

☐ Once a book is well known, use it for simple cloze activities. Mask a word and ask 'What do you think this word is?' (If the book is well known, children will usually give you the word in the text, but accept any response that makes sense.) For some children this activity can be extended by asking a more open-ended question like 'What else could it say?'

☐ Write part of the text on card with some words deleted. (Choose words which you think children will be able to recognise, or which you want to focus on as useful sight words.) Put the deleted words onto small cards. In groups or pairs the children place the words in the appropriate spaces.

☐ Write wall stories with the whole class which innovate on the story.

Developing sight words

☐ Build up a sight vocabulary from classroom labels, class-made books and wall stories, the children's own writing, and written versions of songs and poems which are already known orally. A large sight vocabulary is very important for successful early reading and supports the development of other reading skills. Learning sight words in isolation may be difficult for English speaking children, even though they have the advantage of understanding the words as spoken, but second language learners are likely to find lists of isolated words particularly difficult to understand or learn. They need the support of a context for meaning, and so sight words should be developed from within whole text.

☐ Help children to develop strategies for word attack when they are unable to recognise a word, such as: *go back and read from the beginning of the sentence, and/ or read to the end of the sentence ... check the first letter(s) ... then make a guess.* Children should be able to articulate what to do when they are stuck.

☐ Use 'word cards' for high frequency structure words, for words that children need to write frequently and for words that they get stuck on. Write each word on a strip of card, and on the back use the word in a sentence given to you by the child concerned. Children try to read the word as a sight word, but if they can't, they turn over the card and read the sentence. They are almost always able to read the word in the context of the sentence and so nearly always experience success. They will eventually be able to read the word as a sight word, but until they are able to do so, they continue to use the prompt provided by the context. This also models a good reading strategy: *if you can't read a word, read the rest of the sentence to help you.* The cards can be kept by individual children and read at home. If you have a language master in your school, children can run the words and sentences through the machine for further oral/aural support.

Teaching letter-sound relationships

☐ Aim to demonstrate sound-symbol relationships within a context of known sight words or recognised sentences. The importance of context extends to the teaching of phonological awareness! Sounds in isolation become very distorted and hard to remember because they are abstract. Working from whole meaningful sentences and words is much easier than beginning with isolated sounds and then trying to blend them. In addition, children who speak another language may not 'hear' or recognise some of the sounds of English, or may confuse similar sounds.

For example, within a familiar shared book frame a sentence which the children will recognise, then frame a word and finally frame a letter.

> One day an old woman was cleaning her house when she found an old silver coin.

'My, oh my,' she wondered, 'what shall I spend it on?'

One day an old ⟦woman⟧ was cleaning her house when she found an old silver coin.
'My, oh my,' she wondered, 'what shall I spend it on?'

One day an old ⟦w⟧oman was cleaning her house when she found an old silver coin.
'My, oh my', she wondered, 'what shall I spend it on?'

☐ Whenever possible, encourage children to develop their own generalisations about letter-sound relationships inductively, through words they are already able to read as sight words. If children are able, through shared readings, to read the text above, they can be helped to arrive at their own generalisations about what letter and sound is common to the words *woman, when, wondered* and *what.*

Developing phonic knowledge through known sight words follows two important principles: that of teaching the parts of language within a context, and that of building from the known to the unknown. Nevertheless there may be some children who at times will benefit from a more deductive approach, where a letter-sound relationship is presented and examples given. This may be more appropriate for some children who are already literate in their first language and have developed sophisticated concepts of print.

Remember, however, that English has forty-four sounds, represented by the twenty-six letters, and because of the complications of the spelling system, generalisations about letter-sound relationships will only lead to possibilities, not to certainties!

☐   Another way to develop phonic awareness of initial sounds is by making 'consonant boxes'. Children sort a number of small objects (a pencil, a pen, a pin, a toy car, a cup, a coin) into the appropriate consonant boxes (a box labelled P and one labelled C) depending on the initial sound of the word.

Using children's own writing

☐   The most meaningful words for children are likely to be those they use in their own spoken and written language. Rewrite class stories onto strips of cardboard and mix them up.

| Yesterday we all went to the zoo. |
| We saw lots of animals. |
| First we saw the monkeys. |
| They were very funny |
| and we all laughed a lot. |

Children can reconstruct the story in groups, in pairs or individually.

☐   As a further activity the sentences can be cut into words and reconstructed. It is a good idea to cut out the words without any margin around them, so that children have to remember to space them out as they reconstruct the sentence.

Developing fluency in reading

☐   Use taped readings as a listening post activity. Record a story or other text onto tape which the children listen to while following the written text. This provides visual and aural input for individual children, provides a model of pronunciation and demonstrates the link between the spoken word and print. Children can stop and rewind the tape at any point, so that they are able to control the listening sessions. Encourage children to join in the reading at some point.

☐ Use 'shadowed reading'. This is a very useful strategy for children who are 'failed' readers because the support it offers enables them to be successful, read aloud fluently and read at a higher level than they would normally be able to achieve. It also provides a model of the stress and intonation patterns of English.

Sit slightly behind and to the side of the child with the book in front of the child. Read the whole book to the child. Then reread a part of the book (perhaps a page) several times at normal speed, encouraging the child to join in only as he or she feels able. With the first few readings you will be *leading* the child, who at no point should be left to struggle. The child 'shadows' you as you are reading. As he or she starts to read with confidence, decrease your involvement by lowering your voice and gradually no longer leading.

☐ Occasionally use timed readings to encourage children who read word by word to read more fluently. Ask them to summarise what they have read, to skim for the main idea, or to scan for specific information.

Reading in the content areas — extending the semantic context

The following strategies are particularly useful for older readers and are especially relevant for reading within the content areas, although many could be adapted for narrative texts or for younger children.

Before reading

☐ Discuss with children what they already know about the topic.

☐ Talk about the text before reading, ensuring that you introduce much of the new vocabulary and language structures. Avoid presenting material 'cold'.

☐ Help children to predict what content words are likely to be in the text. Extend their knowledge of the kind of vocabulary that might occur and the words that are likely to be found together (collocation). For example, a book about bees is likely to contain the words *hive, queen, worker, nest, honey, comb, nectar*. Word association tasks before reading the text — such as brainstorming words that are likely to occur together through collocation — will help children to predict successfully and increase fluency.

☐ Aim to develop knowledge and concepts related to the topic in general instead of 'pre-teaching' single passages. Remember that most words have no fixed meaning, but rather a range of meanings depending on the topic and the context. (Think of the word *difference* in its day-to-day context and in its maths context, or the word *determine* in *water determined where people chose to settle* and *she is a very determined person*.) Simply presenting and teaching new vocabulary before reading a text will not necessarily lead to the learning of the concept behind a word, or to improved reading comprehension.

☐   Develop word banks and display vocabulary about topics you are studying.

☐   Give children focus questions before they read.

☐   Use barrier crossword puzzles to focus on spelling and defining key content words (see p. 40).

During and after reading

☐   Use titles, headings and sub-headings to make predictions about what a text might contain.

☐   Get groups of children to represent the text through diagrams or flow charts. Representing ideas and their relationships diagrammatically helps to provide a structure for surveying and reading the text.

☐   Use information transfer activities, where groups or pairs of children construct tables, charts or graphs to represent the information within the text. Or provide the headings on a chart and allow the children to fill in the information.

☐   Provide 'true or false' statements or 'fact or opinion' statements relating to the text. The children must decide which they are. Or have children construct their own 'true or false' statements and exchange them with others.

Focusing on the language systems

Although it is important to develop a reader's understanding of the semantic framework in which a text has been written, we should not neglect the fact that language itself is a major factor in second language reading. The following strategies focus particularly on the structure of the language.

☐   Cut up known sentences into words (for example, from a previous shared book) and mix them up. In groups, pairs or individually, children reorder the words into sentences.

☐   Cut up a paragraph into sentence strips and mix them up. Children reorder the sentences into a coherent sequence.

☐   Cut two short texts into sentences and mix them up. Children unscramble the intermingled texts.

Cloze activities

Use cloze activities as a teaching strategy. (Cloze has sometimes been associated with testing and its full teaching potential has not always been realised.) Normally cloze activities are better used with pairs or groups so that children can compare and discuss their choices. This gives you an opportunity to talk to children about the reasons for their choices, thus helping to make the reading process explicit. Cloze will also give you a good idea of the sorts of reading strategies that individual children are using, such as whether they are using backward and forward referencing.

There is a great variety of cloze activities. Published cloze passages may be useful for indicating general levels of reading ability, but teacher-designed cloze activities are much more useful because they can be tailored to the needs of the children and to suit specific diagnostic and teaching purposes.

Traditional cloze has deletions about every seventh word. They therefore fall randomly and do not focus on any particular language item. They are useful in determining whether children are gaining the overall meaning of the text, and whether the text is at an appropriate level.

Syntactic cloze deletes structure words (see p. 73) of one type, such as all the pronouns, or all the connectives, or perhaps word endings. These deletions may be particularly difficult for second language learners because they relate closely to the structure of the language.

Semantic cloze deletes content words (see p. 72). These will probably relate to the specific vocabulary of the topic.

Graphophonic cloze deletes some letters of some words, perhaps the initial cluster or ending, or some letters of letter clusters.

Deletions may be made in a variety of ways.

- Leave uniform gaps for all words deleted.

- Leave gaps to represent the letters missing.

- Leave gaps which indicate the first letter of the deleted word.

- Delete as usual, but also provide a list of the words which have been deleted (with or without distractors).

- Mask a word using 'Post-it' labels, perhaps during a shared book experience, while children predict what it might be.

- Put the text on an overhead projector, cover a word while children discuss the most suitable choice, and then reveal it.

- Use oral/aural cloze. Read a text aloud while the children follow a written version; the written version contains deletions which the children fill in as they hear the words. (This can also be done as a listening post activity using a taped passage.)

Another approach is to expose the text on an overhead, bit by bit, so that children can predict what they think it might say.

Making links in text — understanding cohesion

Cohesion is what makes the difference between a list of unrelated sentences and a group of sentences that together form a coherent whole. The following sentences bear no relationship to each other.

> Typhoons are strong winds. Canberra is the capital of Australia. Koalas are marsupials. Every day he wished he could see his home again. However she hard she tried, she was never able to beat her record.

However, the sentences below, adapted from the beginning of *The Little Drummer Girl* (John Le Carré), link to create a coherent paragraph. The major cohesive links have been indicated.

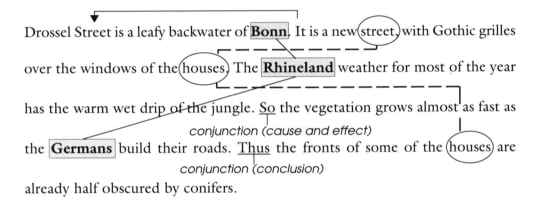

Drossel Street is a leafy backwater of **Bonn**. It is a new street, with Gothic grilles over the windows of the houses. The **Rhineland** weather for most of the year has the warm wet drip of the jungle. So the vegetation grows almost as fast as
conjunction (cause and effect)
the **Germans** build their roads. Thus the fronts of some of the houses are
conjunction (conclusion)
already half obscured by conifers.

One of the things that a fluent reader does is to carry meaning across chunks of text. Less fluent readers tend not to do this, but to focus instead on much smaller units of meaning, such as individual words. Being able to carry an idea right through a text is dependent on being able to process the cohesive links between sentences.

A native speaker has an intuitive understanding of how cohesion operates, but second language learners may not have developed this understanding fully. Helping readers to be aware of cohesive links will help them to see the wholeness of a text and so understand it more easily.

Halliday and Hasan (1976) have identified five ways in which English creates cohesive ties and each of them is described below, together with the particular difficulty it may cause for second language learners.

Reference

◀   ◀

A tall black figure was outside Sophie's house. The figure turned and faced her

◀   ◀   ◀

window, and then he walked on. He came to Mr. Goochey's house and there

◀

he stopped.   (adapted from *The BFG* by Roald Dahl)

Reference words point to something in the text. They usually (but not always) point *back* to something that has already been mentioned. They include words like *he, she, it, his, hers, him, her, they, their, them, here, there, the* (when referring to something already mentioned), *this, those, that,* etc.

Second language learners may not recognise the relationship between the reference word and the referent as they are reading, and may not make it clear in their writing.

Conjunction

C   C

He walked all day although he was exhausted. Finally he stopped outside a

C   C

small hotel in a village. If he went in, someone might recognise him, but

C   C

unless he stopped to rest he would get no further. So, hoping he would remain

unrecognised, he opened the door.

Conjunctions are often key words in the linking and organisation of ideas. They include words like *and, but, because, so, unless, although, if, however, nevertheless, therefore,* etc. One group of linking words has to do with sequencing ideas in time (time connectives) and includes words and phrases like *and, and then, before, after, later, the next day, millions of years later, afterwards,* etc.

Conjunctions link ideas but they do more than that. They also help the reader to interpret what comes next in the text, or to predict the sort of meaning that will follow. Think of how the conjunctions *although, but* and *because* help the reader to predict how these sentences are likely to end.

Although the light was red, the car ... (didn't stop).

The light was red, but the car ... (didn't stop).

Because the light was red, the car ... (stopped).

Conjunctions are therefore key words in helping readers to recognise and interpret the main ideas of the text.

> *Many second language learners do not control a sufficient range of conjunctions and connectives, and this means they are less likely to read with understanding or recognise the main points of a text. It is also likely that their writing will sound less fluent or unstructured.*

Substitution

                                                S

He was given a new bike for his birthday. His old one was too small for him.

Here *one* has been substituted for *bike*.

> *Second language learners may not recognise that both words refer to the same thing.*

Ellipsis

Some cats like cheese but some don't⟨⟨.

He sat down, ⟨ stood up and then ⟨ sat down again.

In the first example, *like cheese* has been omitted and has to be supplied by the reader. In the second example, there is ellipsis of the word *he*. Ellipsis is part of the structure of English; it is not 'lazy' or 'careless' speech.

> *Second language learners may not be able to supply what is not there, or may not recognise that anything has been omitted. In either case they may be unable to comprehend the text. They will also be unable to use this structure in their writing, which may cause it to sound unnecessarily 'wordy'.*

Lexical cohesion

They were now in a country of thick (forests) and rushing (rivers). The giant had

definitely **slowed** down and was now **running** more normally although normal was a silly word to describe a **galloping** giant. He **leapt** over a dozen rivers. He went **rattling** through a great forest then down into a valley and up over a range of hills, and soon he was **galloping** over a desolate wasteland that was not quite of this earth.   (adapted from *The BFG* by Roald Dahl)

Many of the content words within this passage fall into two groups, those to do with movement and those to do with the physical aspects of the scene. These strings of related words help to hold the text together. Understanding them and seeing the relationship between them also depends very much on a reader's world knowledge.

> *Second language learners may not have this amount of semantic variety within their vocabulary.*

Seeing the links

Understanding how cohesion works will help you, as a teacher, to:

- see why children may not be understanding what they read
- recognise potential difficulties within a text
- see why children's writing may not sound fluent (even though there may be no obvious error)
- devise appropriate reading and writing strategies.

It will also help you to evaluate texts, particularly those that appear to be simple. The example below comes from a natural history text (discussed in Anderson 1982) which was intended for very young readers.

> An insect flies into the web. It struggles. The spider comes running down. It binds the insect with silk. Then it bites it with its fangs and poisons it. If the spider is hungry it eats the insect. If not, it keeps it for later.

This text seems simple and easy to read. In fact the number of uses of the word *it* (referring to both the spider and the fly) makes the text unnaturally complicated, especially for a reader who is not already aware of the process being described.

Making children aware of how cohesion works does not mean that it should be considered in isolation, or that it is necessary for children to know the terminology given here. Because cohesion relates to *whole text*, it can only be understood within a context. (Imagine the difficulty of explaining — and understanding — words like *however, although* or *but* in isolation.) The following are some examples of how the system of cohesion can be demonstrated to children.

☐ Use shared book experiences to focus on all aspects of cohesion, especially reference and conjunction. Use a cloze technique and mask some of the words, or, informally and as you are reading, point to reference words like *he* and *she* and ask 'Who is this talking about?'

☐ Use cloze and delete one type of cohesive link, as suggested earlier.

☐ Use modelled writing and writing conferences to draw children's attention to the links between sentences.

☐ Cut up a paragraph into sentences and ask groups or pairs of children to reconstruct it. Asking 'How do you know?' and encouraging children to explain their choice of order is a useful way of talking about language in a meaningful context.

☐ Focus on particular conjunctions by building up a text with the children. For example, begin a story and invite suggestions as to what might come next:

> Once upon a time there lived a monster. *Although* he was very large and looked very fierce, he ....

Because cohesion is not a very visible language system and is one which is intuitively understood by native speakers, it is easy to overlook the difficulties it may cause for second language learners. Conjunctions in particular are often overlooked as a potential area of difficulty, and we need to check that these words are understood when they occur in text. The child who writes *although the light was red the car stopped* could, when reading, miss the point of an entire paragraph where comprehension hinges on understanding the word *although*. Making the system of cohesion more explicit to children will help them to:

- carry meaning at the level of whole text
- use forward and backward referencing as they read
- see the organisation of a text by recognising key words such as conjunctions
- write more fluently.

Collaborative reading: a group reading strategy

Collaborative or shared reading is a useful strategy to use when children are reading for information, and it is also a way of organising children with different reading abilities to work together.

You may need to enlist the help of your librarian to help provide four or five readings on the same topic. (These can be at varying levels to suit the different readers in your class. Label, colour-code or number the readings, for example from

1 to 5. All the 1's will be the same, all the 2's the same and so on.) In groups of four or five, the children are each given a different reading, which they read silently. They then make notes, summarising the main points. Finally each child shares what he or she has read with the group, while the other members listen and take notes if they wish. The group therefore has the benefit of five sources of information about the topic.

A variation on this, which will help less confident readers, is to add an initial step. Begin by grouping all the '1' readers together, all the '2's and so on. Each child in the group therefore has the same reading. After reading their text they discuss the main points with other members of the group, so that they become 'experts' in this reading. After this the children move into their mixed groups and proceed as described above.

Collaborative reading has a number of advantages.

- Since each child is responsible to the rest of the group for providing the information in his or her reading, there is a real purpose for reading.

- It encourages children to listen to each other and to work cooperatively and collaboratively.

- It is possible for children of different reading abilities to work together at levels which suit them individually.

- It integrates talking, listening and writing with reading.

- It provides a structure to support less confident children and enables them to participate on an equal basis within the group.

- It is a child-centred way of presenting information.

Reflective reading

This chapter has focused on two aspects of reading: learning to read and reading to learn. While the development of the skills of reading must always play a major part in any reading program, we must not forget the readers themselves — potentially critical and creative readers with a love of reading and an appreciation of literature. Reading also has an aesthetic function, and we will be doing young readers — whether first or second language learners — a great disservice if we do not include as part of the reading program books which demonstrate to them the metaphoric, poetic and lyrical qualities of language.

With thoughtful questioning and discussion, children can respond at a personal level to the imagery, analogy and universal themes which characterise the best of what is written for young readers. Empathising with characters and drawing analogies with their own experiences will help children make sense of the significant events in their own lives.

Using literature, children can be encouraged to think widely and creatively through the types of questions we generate with them. Questions can invite an alternative perspective — *What might have happened if ...?* Or they may require critical comment on the events of the story — *Do you think that was the right thing to do? Would you have done that? Why?* Or they may focus on the writer's use of language — *How did you feel when ...? How did the writer make you feel like that?*

At a time when education, and language in particular, is viewed increasingly in rationalist and economic terms, we need to give children the time to reflect critically, creatively and with enthusiasm on what they read, and encourage reading for personal growth and pleasure.

Reading and language development

The development of any one of the four major functions of language facilitates and is supported by development in the other three. Reading cannot be seen in isolation from listening, speaking and writing, and a reading program must include opportunities to use language in these other ways in reading-related activities. This is especially important for second language learners, who need the support of other language contexts that will feed into their reading.

The great majority of children will be reading by the end of their first year at school if teachers expect this and plan for it. Of course not all children develop reading skills at the same rate, but it is important that a child who is not reading after a year in school is 'tracked' and given extra support during the second year. This does not imply that such children are 'remedial' readers, but that intervention is necessary to prevent early failure and low self-esteem. The ability to read is fundamental to learning, and the earlier a child acquires this skill, the greater will be his or her capacity for learning.

Again this is especially important for second language learners. Often their English language models are restricted to what they hear in school. Once they are able to read in English, their language environment will be enriched because of the greatly increased number and variety of language models available to them. There is a 'chicken and egg' effect. While increased language competence enhances reading ability, reading certainly increases language competence.

CHAPTER EIGHT

Learning to Listen and Getting the Sounds Right

This chapter discusses strategies for improving children's listening skills, and includes suggestions for helping children who have difficulties with some aspects of English pronunciation.

Listening

Reading and listening are closely related language processes. Good readers are usually good listeners, and the listening process breaks down for similar reasons as the reading process.

Like reading, effective listening requires the listener to be active and thinking. Understanding what you hear depends on your background knowledge of the topic or situation and your knowledge of the language itself. While reading requires knowing the symbols of written language, listening requires recognising the sounds of the language. The information sources for comprehension in listening are therefore parallel to those for reading.

Specially designed listening material is useful to provide practice for specific skills, but many of the best listening activities are those where listening is integrated with speaking, reading and writing. All the ideas for communicative and collaborative activities in this book involve listening. The dictogloss procedure described on p. 108-09 is a good example of an integrated listening activity.

There is a danger that listening will only be planned for incidentally because it is a less tangible skill, and so it's a good idea to program for it to occur regularly. The next section contains examples of how listening can be integrated with other language activities. Aim to use a variety of sources for listening — audio tapes, videos, teachers, other adults and the children themselves.

Integrating listening activities

☐ Encourage questioning for clarification while children are involved in collaborative activities. The barrier games described in Chapter 2 provide opportunities for pairs of children to question each other when the information given by one child has not been clear.

☐ Model questioning. Encourage children to respond actively when they do not understand something — reassure them that asking for clarification is something everyone needs to do on occasions. In the classroom many children become used to never fully understanding what is said to them. If we wish them to take responsibilty for their own learning and understandings, then they must be provided with the language that will help them to do so. It may be necessary to model some of the language used to ask for clarification. This is very important and powerful classroom language because it helps children to become active, independent and critical learners.

'When you said ..., did you mean ...?'

'Excuse me, what do you mean by ...?'

'Could you tell me again ...?'

'I didn't understand the bit where ....'

'Could you repeat that please?'

☐ Plan activities where there is a purpose for listening. The immediate function for listening should be clear. Children could:

- take notes from a news bulletin

- carry out an activity from a set of spoken instructions

- extract one point of view from a debate they have listened to

- listen for differences between two stories which differ only in minor details.

☐ Use collaborative listening situations, such as the dictogloss technique, where children are given responsibility for the learning of others as well as themselves. Often it is possible to adapt something you are already doing. For example, when children are watching a video or a television program, divide them into pairs. Give each pair two different sets of focus questions. The children each listen for their specific information and at the end share this with their partners.

☐ During group discussions demonstrate to children how to listen actively by reflecting back to the speaker what has been said, using structures like *so you're saying that* ..., *you think that* ..., *you mean that* ..... This is a way of checking that a speaker's message has been understood properly. It also encourages children to listen to each other and gives them opportunities to summarise what a speaker has said.

☐ On occasions try speaking much more quietly than you normally do, and warn children that you will give instructions only once!

Some focused listening activities

When necessary, focus on more specific skills of listening. Some children may have difficulty in hearing — and therefore producing — the sounds, stress patterns and intonation patterns of English.

☐ Clap a rhythm which children copy.

☐ Practice aural recognition of the rhythms of English. Get children to clap the rhythm of poems, rhymes and chants. As not all syllables in English are stressed equally, make sure that children make a distinction by clapping unstressed syllables more quietly:

Hick — or — y   dick — or — y   dock

CLAP   clap   clap   CLAP   clap   clap   CLAP

This is much more successful if you use rhymes which have been learned aurally. (Reading rhymes aloud focuses children's attention onto the print rather than the sound.)

☐ Play listening games like 'Chinese Whispers'. With children sitting in a circle, you whisper something quietly to one child, who then whispers it to the next child, and so on. (The message should stay the same but rarely does!)

☐ Play minimal pair games. Minimal pairs are words which are identical except for one sound, such as *tree/three, nine/line, bin/pin*. If these sounds do not occur in the mother tongue, or if only one does, it is likely that the difference will not be heard in English. This will interfere with children's comprehension and pronunciation. Focus their attention on the sounds that are confused by writing pairs of words on opposite sides of a blackboard or large sheet of paper. Alternatively use two drawings such as those shown below. Say the words at random while the children point to what they think you are saying.

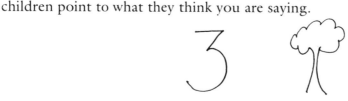

Listening and pronunciation

Pronunciation is included here because the focused listening activities discussed above lead naturally into pronunciation practice. Most young children learn to sound like their peers very quickly; usually pronunciation is not a major difficulty or does not remain so for very long. Depending on their age when they begin learning English, some children will continue to speak with an 'accent'. But as a general rule, unless a child's speech is interfering with communication, it is much better to spend time on general language development rather than on isolated speech activities aimed at improving prounciation. However, where speech is a barrier to communication and the child is no longer in the very early stages of English, it may be necessary to devise some more specific activities.

Stress and intonation

Initially concentrate on general fluency and speech rhythms. Once a speaker has mastered the stress and intonation patterns of English, pronunciation difficulties with specific sounds are often much less apparent. Some languages have very different stress patterns from English; some stress every syllable equally — a characteristic which may be transferred into English. (Read that last sentence giving equal weighting to each syllable and it may remind you of the speech of some second language learners.)

The stress patterns of English mean that many unstressed words (which are often structure rather than content words) are pronounced differently in continuous speech from the way they are said alone. Note how different the following words sound when they are said in isolation and within a sentence:

was   He was standing by the gate.

from   I came from Italy.

some   They ate some lunch.

When structure words like these are unstressed, they 'weaken' or change the sound of their vowel. This is not 'careless' but a feature of normal English speech.

☐ Model the stress and intonation patterns of English through jingles and rhymes, beginning with clapping the rhythm. Teach children the rhymes *orally* so that they attend to the sounds rather than to print.

☐ Concentrate in particular on the linking sounds between words where these occur. In the phrase *not at all*, for instance, the *t* sounds are clearly articulated so that at normal speed it sounds like *no-ta-tall*. This is a difficulty for children whose first language (such as Cantonese) does not have voiced consonants at the end of words. Demonstrate phrases like this by breaking up the words: e.g. *tha-tis* (= that is), *wan-tit* (= want it), *foun-dit* (= found it). Once children are able to link words appropriately, their language will immediately sound more fluent and less accented.

☐ Sometimes stress and intonation patterns are more easily mastered if you demonstrate them by beginning from the end of a line, keeping stress patterns consistent:

the *hill*

up the *hill*

went *up* the *hill*

Jill went *up* the *hill*

and *Jill* went *up* the *hill*

Jack and *Jill* went *up* the *hill*

Practising 'problem' sounds

☐ Use minimal pair exercises to check that children can hear the sound in a word. Often teaching children to hear differences is enough to enable them to produce the sound. Practise listening and saying the sound in a sentence as well as in a word, since it's important that they understand that the sound makes a difference in *meaning*:

He dropped the bin.

He dropped the pin.

☐ Let children look in a mirror while saying a word or a sound. For example, the *th* in English occurs in very few languages and many second language learners find it difficult. Using a mirror helps them to see how the sound is made.

☐ Draw attention to the difference between voiced and unvoiced consonants if children do not already make the distinction. For example, the sounds *b*, *d* and *g* all require the voice to be used. Their unvoiced equivalents are *p*, *t* and *k*. Demonstrate the difference to children by holding a piece of paper close to your mouth. The unvoiced sounds require much more breath and will make the paper move.

☐ Where *n* and *l* are confused, demonstrate the difference by getting children to touch their noses while saying the sounds. *n* is produced using the air through the nose, and vibration can be felt there.

☐ Pay attention to word endings, especially -*ed* endings. Regular past tense endings in English often end with the sound of two or more consonants: for example, *jumped* (ends with the sound *mpt*), *dropped* (ends with the sound *pt*), or *grabbed* (ends with the sound *bd*). Not all languages have consonant clusters like these or end words in this way. Consequently, because children are not used to these sounds, they may not hear the endings, may not say them and therefore do not write them. Leaving the endings off words in writing may be a listening and pronunciation problem as much as a writing and grammatical problem!

While there is a place for specific pronunciation teaching for some children, remember that many speech exercises become meaningless in isolation. It is better to develop good speech habits within normal classroom activities, such as through drama, poetry or readers' theatre. Most pronunciation difficulties do not last with children beginning English during their primary years, and unless there is a genuine speech problem, major intervention is rarely necessary.

CHAPTER NINE

The Writing Program

Finding a direction

The shells are much littlebit lit. The wool are very lit. The cot are very very lit. The roke are much littlebit hever. The chalk are very lit.

Katia wrote this piece to record a maths activity while she was in Year 1. It is quite an impressive achievement, particularly for someone who had been learning English for just over a year. Her writing indicates both her understanding of the maths task and her ability to record what she has done. The comparisons she makes between the weights of the various materials, although not expressed accurately in grammatical terms, are quite clear. Most of the spelling is correct, and the approximations indicate that she is developing an understanding of sound/symbol relationships (e.g. *lit* for *light, hever* for *heavy*).

But this piece of writing is also a valuable guide for her teacher's future programming. It indicates in particular two language areas where Katia needs some extra support and intervention.

>**The distinction between 'mass' and 'count' nouns.** English makes a distinction between things which are countable (such as *buttons, pencils* and *books* or, in this case, *rocks* and *shells*) and those materials which are not (such as *grass, sugar* and *flour* or, in this case, *wool* and *chalk*). This distinction manifests itself throughout the English language (*how **many** books* but *how **much** flour, the shells **are*** but *the chalk **is***, etc.).

>**Expressing comparison.** Katia is not using conventional expressions for comparison (such as *lighter, heavier, much lighter, much heavier, very light, very heavy, quite heavy*, etc.).

Both language areas could be modelled and used in a variety of cross-curriculum situations, where Katia could work with a competent English speaker as a language model. Further maths activities could be set up to focus specifically on this language. Following a recipe and weighing and measuring cooking ingredients, or setting up a shop in the classroom would both require the use of mass and count nouns.

But it is often much more difficult than this to see the kind of help that is needed. The second piece (shown overleaf) is from Daniel, a Year 6 child who has had all his education in Australia but speaks another language at home.

It is obvious that Daniel has considerable difficulty in expressing himself in English, but it is much harder to be explicit about what these difficulties are. Responding to a piece of writing only at the level of intuition is unhelpful, because it does not enable us to give useful feedback to the child or decide on the most appropriate learning strategies. Knowing where to begin to help a child is often the hardest part of developing a writing program. The next section suggests a possible 'way in' to this task.

Finding a starting point: a framework for analysing written products

This section describes a procedure for analysing written language, but it should be seen as only a part of a total assessment process. The information gained from analysing the products of language should be supplemented by a teacher's informal observations and interactions with each child. To build up a picture of a learner we also need to draw on our knowledge of his or her attitude to writing and the processes he or she uses.

THE Problems of migrants in australia

well one early morning obaut 5o clock we all lejt our place and went to the airoport. to pitk. my unkle and when we reached to the airoport. we saw him outside of the airoport and it was he's first time. in a Australia. and we took him to our place. and he saw a lot of people working in shop. and when we reached there and we went inside and my unkle said you got a nice place anb that jist time seen my unkle. and when sat down on chair my mother was pepering a cup of cojser and we took obaut how did do m Italy. and my aunkle told obout that at Italy. isald jo dea of thing arp he is to dea. _to and on next day we went to shop and my unkle wants to a pair of Spushater shoe and Ae said how munsh is this shoe. and shoe man said it is $97.49 each and that to dea than in Italy.

Daniel's text.

However, an analysis of children's current language use is essential in providing information about specific language needs. As with the assessment of spoken language (see Chapter 4), the assessment of writing should be seen primarily as a data-gathering exercise for the teacher, not as a way of ranking children.

Opposite is a framework for analysing writing in terms of its linguistic features. For this kind of analysis a piece of writing needs to be unconferenced. It need not be a first draft, but it should represent what the child is able to do *without help*. The specimen sheet has been filled out in response to a report (below) written by Tomi, a Year 6 child who had been in Australia about a year at the time of writing.

Cell and Body Structure:
Shark's body is elongated, rounded and tapering to strongly tail. In difference from other fish shark does not have bones but it has cartilages in skeleton. It has a few types of fins like steadies, tailfins, ventral fins, triangular dorsal fin and pectoral fins.

Body Covering:
Shark's body is covering by coarse skin. On the skin there are small toothlike scales. Those scales make shark's skin rough. The skin of shark is using like a sandpaper for polishing wood.

Movement:
Sharks travel a great burst of the speed. Scientists have recorded a blue shark

WRITING RECORD FOR ...Tomi...

Date of writing / General features	Text type	Overall organisation	Cohesion		Vocabulary	Sentence structure	Punctuation	Spelling
			Connectives	Pronoun reference				
26.4.91 Report on Sharks • Used information from library – good research skills • Expanded main ideas, information is clear	Report (this was set topic)	• good • used subtitles but no main title • needed general classific- ation at beginning	• used <u>instead if</u>. <u>but</u> <u>so</u>, <u>because</u>	• switched between sing. + plural: '<u>they</u> will <u>sink</u> because <u>it</u> ...'	• excellent for topic • note 'strongly tail'	• needs help in expressing generalisations (a/the omitted – 'shark's body' 'the skin of shark') • note: 'in difference from', 'is covering by' 'a great burst of the speed'	• good (is he clear that shark's is singular? • doesn't (inapprop- riate register)	good check <u>swiming</u> <u>wich</u> <u>cresent</u> <u>trough</u>

wich has travel sixty-nine km. per hour. Shark's body is shaped like that so it can move trough the water like a torpedo. It has a cresent shaped tail which gives it a power for swiming. Sharks lack the swim-bladder. Instead they have a liver with a lot of oil in. That oil is lighter than the water so shark doesn't sink. They swim constantly. If they stop moving they will sink because it has no swim-bladder. Sharks must move from the moment they are born.

The writing is considered 'top down': that is, by looking first at the text type or genre the child has chosen and its appropriateness for the writing task; then at its overall structure, its cohesiveness and the sentence grammar; and finally at the spelling and punctuation. The fact that these are considered last does not mean they are unimportant, but simply that concentrating on the more 'surface' areas of spelling and punctuation does little to substantially change a less successful piece of writing. Correcting the spelling of Daniel's text, for example, would not greatly improve it for the reader.

In using the analysis sheet, consider each column in relation to the types of questions suggested below. You can also refer to the major language features of each text type which are listed on pp. 106-07.

General features

- Is the meaning clear?

- Are the main ideas developed/expanded/elaborated/relevant?

- Does the text show an understanding of the purpose for writing?

- Does it reflect the writer's other language experiences (e.g. what has been read, discussed, seen)?

- What is the length of the piece compared to previous writing?

- When appropriate (e.g. in a narrative), does the writing show imagination and creativity?

- Is there deliberate experimentation (e.g. a humorous send-up of a report)?

Text type/genre/form

- What type of text is this (e.g. personal recount, narrative, information report, newspaper report, explanation, discussion, personal or formal letter, play script, poem, etc.)?

- Is the type of text appropriate to the purpose? (Note that while the title of Daniel's text suggests an information report or a discussion, what he has written is a recount.)

Overall organisation

- Is the writing as a whole structured appropriately? (See the information on text type features on pp. 106-07.)

- Is the layout appropriate (e.g. use of headings and subheadings, basic conventions of play scripts, etc.)?

Text cohesion

- Are connectives used to link ideas?
- Are apppropriate connectives used? (These will vary depending on text type.)
- Do pronouns have a clear referent (e.g. is it clear who *he/she/they* refers to)?
- Are pronouns used correctly (e.g. does *he/she* refer to male/female)?

Vocabulary

- Is this appropriate to the text type (e.g. the use of technical vocabulary within a report, or emotive, descriptive vocabulary within a narrative or personal recount)?
- Is there semantic variety where it is appropriate (e.g. the use of alternatives to *said* in a narrative)?

Sentence structure/grammar

- Is this correct (e.g. tense, subject-verb agreement, word order, use of prepositions)?
- Is there a variety of sentence types — simple and complex?

Punctuation

- Is this adequate for the writing?
- Is it used correctly?
- Does it enhance the readability of the writing?

Spelling

- Is conventional spelling used?
- Where there are approximations, what does the writer know about spelling (e.g. knows letters within word — *wsa* for *was;* has phonetic knowledge — *lukt* for *looked*)?
- Is the writer making use of environmental print within the classroom?

These questions can also serve as a structure for a subsequent conference with the writer. (The questions are of course intended for the teacher.) Comments can often be jotted down onto the analysis sheet while the conference is going on, which helps save time.

If several pieces of writing are analysed in this way over a term, a profile of the language use of the learner builds up, and in particular recurring difficulties are more easily identified. It is also possible to begin to see where there may be gaps in the learner's use of language. It will become obvious, for example, if a child never attempts to write non-narrative text.

Individual language profiles like this are also the building blocks of a class profile. A class profile collates the information gained from all the individual profiles and is therefore a summary of the language needs of the whole class. The class profile identifies those language needs which are:

- common to the whole class

- common to some children

- specific to individuals.

A class profile might look something like this.

LANGUAGE PROFILE FOR YEAR 4
(adapted from Anstey and Bull 1989)

All children

Tend to concentrate on recount and narrative, rarely choosing non-narrative genres; similarly narrow reading interests.

Tend to copy chunks of text from reference books to complete report writing.

Use a limited range of time connectives in narrative writing (mainly *and then*).

Groups

Daniel, Carlos, Rebecca, Vivienne, Maria, Christian: have difficulty with story structure (mainly no resolution).

Daniel, Maria, William, Monique: have difficulty expressing generalisations in report writing.

Daniel, John, Susan, Kim, Hannah, Marco: past tense mistakes.

Individuals

Gayle: needs help with proof reading and spelling strategies.

William: choice of topic very limited.

Kim: needs help with spelling strategies.

Lee: just beginning to write in English.

This grouping helps the teacher to establish 'skills groups', which are groups of children who have particular language needs in common, and who will come together at specific times for teacher-directed activities aimed at focusing on certain skills or language areas. They are *not* ability groups and will be regularly disbanded as the skills are mastered and new needs are assessed. Skills groups are also a useful organisational option where there is a second teacher (such as an ESL teacher) working in the class with you. These groups of children may be those with whom he or she works most closely.

A class profile should provide a starting point for programming. While you will already have certain long-term aims regarding what you would like children to be achieving by the end of the year, the profile will help to set the short-term goals which are prerequisites for these aims to be achieved.

For example, as the teacher of the Year 4 class profiled opposite, one of your long-term aims might be for children to be able to write in a range of text types. The profile makes it clear that most children are having difficulty with certain aspects of narrative writing, in particular with expressing a sequence of events in time. A short-term goal might be for them to develop a range of time connectives that will provide them with alternatives to *and then*, and these are some of the strategies you might adopt.

☐ Read several times a big book in which a range of time connectives is modelled (e.g. *later, the next day, some time after, the next morning*).

☐ Use 'Post-it' strips to mask out these connectives and, as an oral cloze, ask children to predict or recall what was written.

☐ Brainstorm other possibilities for these words and display them in the classroom.

☐ In modelled writing sessions focus on connectives within a whole text ('How else can we say *and then* in this story?').

☐ In group language activities use as cloze exercises short narratives in which connectives are deleted. (Cloze is usually more effective as a teaching strategy if children work on it in pairs or as a group.)

☐ Include a focus on this aspect of narrative writing in individual conferences as necessary.

It should now be apparent that a class profile is closely related to programming and will usually make the programming task far simpler, since it will be clear what focused activities are most relevant for the particular children in your class.

What do bilingual children need to learn about writing?

Much of what bilingual childen have to learn about writing they share with English speaking children, but the aspects of writing described here may be of special relevance.

They need to learn the symbols of the writing system and the relationships between sound and symbols

Children who are literate in their first language may have learned to read and write using another script, such as Chinese, Arabic, Korean, Macedonian or Greek. Some may use a script which is very similar to the Roman script but has different sound/symbol relationships, such as Turkish, where, for example, *c* sounds like the *j* of *jam*. Others may have used the Roman script with the addition of diacritics (accent markers), such as Vietnamese.

Children may also have difficulties with the spelling system of English because of pronunciation differences between languages. Their first language, for example, may not have a near equivalent to a particular English sound, or may have two near equivalents. Being unable to hear the difference between sounds may influence spelling, but this is a result of the child's language experience, not of any hearing or speech deficit. (See Chapter 8 for some suggestions about developing listening skills.)

Punctuation in written language reflects the intonation patterns and pauses of spoken language. Thus an understanding of punctuation partly depends on the writer being able to control the speech patterns of English.

They need to learn how writing differs from speech

Much of the thinking about writing development over the last few years has emphasised the parallels between speech and writing. In many ways the two processes are very similar, particularly in the importance of approximations in moving towards the 'adult' version. A great deal of useful material has been written on implications for the classroom (see, for example, Cambourne and Turbill 1987), and this section should be read with the *processes* of writing in mind.

However, the similarities between the *development* of speech and writing should not obscure their very fundamental differences from a language point of view, which go far beyond the fact that the sounds of speech are represented in letters.

1 Speech tends to rely heavily on reference words (like *this, here, there, it*) which refer to something within view of the speakers: they 'point' to things which are *outside* the actual language. *Put it there next to that other one* depends on the listener seeing what *it, there* and *that other one* refer to. In a piece of written text, reference words like these usually serve a very different function. They would normally be pointing to something which has already been mentioned *within* the text:

> The boy stood beside the tree gazing up at the kite which was tangled in *its* branches. He stood *there* for a long time, wondering how to get *it* down.

Cartoons are an exception to the way reference works in writing. Perhaps the closeness of their language to speech, and its familiarity, partly explains their popularity.

2 Spoken language usually relies on the speaker and listener being in face-to-face contact, which affords them a range of visual support for meaning (such as gesture and facial expression). It also relies on the skills of the listener to cope with things like false starts, changes of tack and incomplete utterances. (If you see spoken language written down exactly as it is said, you will find that grammatically it is actually more complex than written language.) A reader of a written text, on the other hand, cannot ask for clarification if something is not understood. Written language must make everything clear to the reader, and so there is normally a much higher proportion of content words (like nouns, adjectives and verbs). Mature writing is denser than speech (and will sound 'written' even when it is read aloud).

3 Writing requires much more understanding *about* language than speech. Using capitals and full stops involves having some conscious understanding of what a sentence is. The notions of a sentence or a paragraph are abstractions which are irrelevant for a speaker at a conscious level.

The differences between speech and writing help to explain why it is often not enough just to talk about a topic before a child writes about it. Talk helps to clarify ideas and content, but turning talk into writing involves much more. Writing is not the same as speech written down, and most children need a bridge into written text by seeing demonstrations of both the processes and the products of writing.

They need to learn the different text types or genres of English

Text types or genres are culturally determined. The style and tone of a business letter in Spanish, for example, is very different from one in English. The way that genres are organised is not the result of arbitrary rules, but a reflection of the way that a particular language is organised to fulfil specific purposes. There would be a high degree of agreement among English speakers about the essential features of a recipe, because these are what are required within the language in order to organise information effectively for a particular purpose — describing how to cook something.

Each type of text or genre has its own particular language features which a writer must understand. These have to do with:

- the overall structure or organisation (an information report organises information differently from a narrative)

- the order of the parts (in an information report general classification normally precedes detailed description)

- the specific grammatical features (such as the type of connectives, the tense, the type of vocabulary, etc.).

The language features of five genres are briefly described below. For a much fuller description of the language features of various genres, see *Exploring How Texts Work* by Beverly Derewianka (PETA 1990).

The genres described here are best considered as 'prototypes'. Good writers frequently break rules. For example, many of the most creative short stories do not follow the structure suggested below. A writer may play with the order of events, perhaps creating a series of flashbacks or beginning with the resolution of the story. But the deliberate breaking of rules for literary effect is very different from not knowing the rules in the first place, and understanding and controlling the written genres of a culture is part of becoming a creative writer.

All children, whether English speaking or bilingual, need to develop this understanding. Bilingual childen, since they are to varying degrees likely to be less familiar with the written genres of the dominant culture, may need particular support in mastering control of these writing forms. An English speaking child, for example, will need to learn that generalisations are an important way of handling information within a report. Bilingual children may also have to learn how to express the particular grammatical form of a generalisation (e.g. *sharks swim*, not *shark swim*).

The language features of some genre prototypes

Narrative

Content: about specific people and events.
Overall structure: orientation — event(s) — complication — resolution.
Cohesion: especially connnectives which show sequence in time, e.g. *then, later, meanwhile, a few months later.*
Other language demands: probably past tense; variety of verbs for action and feeling; emotive vocabulary intended to make the reader respond in certain ways.

Recount

Content: about specific people and events, but probably personal, e.g. 'My Day at the Zoo'.
Overall structure: orientation — event(s) — conclusion.
Cohesion: as for Narrative.
Other language demands: as for Narrative; writer is 'I'.

Report

Content: about things in general and intended to inform, e.g. 'All about Koalas'.
Overall structure: general classification — description — description.
Cohesion: especially through backward reference, e.g. *Koalas ... they ... they.*
Other language demands: subject-specific (non-emotive) vocabulary; expression of generalisations.

Procedure

Content: about processes and intended to inform, e.g. 'How to Make a Kite', 'The Formation of a Fossil'.
Overall structure: introduction — event — event — (conclusion).
Cohesion: especially connectives which show sequence in time, e.g. *first, second, finally, millions of years later.*

Other language demands: verbs to describe actions, happenings (and, for instructions, the use of 'you' or imperative); subject-specific vocabulary.

Argument

Content: aims to persuade, e.g. 'The Ideal Teacher'.
Overall structure: thesis — argument — argument — conclusion; *or* thesis — arguments — counter arguments — conclusion.
Cohesion: especially connectives for presentation of ideas, e.g. *first, second, however, on the other hand, therefore.*
Other language demands: expressing generalisations; probably subject-specific vocabulary.

Developing effective writers

The best place for teaching genres is in those areas of the curriculum where they naturally occur, such as social studies or science. The teaching of language through context is almost always more successful than teaching it in isolation. There is little evidence that the isolated teaching of rules and structures has any effect on actual language use. The process of writing should occur in all curriculum areas, not only in the language block itself.

There may be some children who will develop the ability to write in a range of genres without planned intervention from the teacher. However, we cannot assume all children will do so, and therefore the development of a range of genres should be a focus for planning within the program.

The following strategies and ideas are aimed at making the processes and products of writing explicit to bilingual children.

☐ Demonstrate writing, both process and product. This can take the form of the teacher modelling the process by writing in front of the class and 'thinking aloud' (*Now what should I put next?*). Or else it may involve a 'joint construction' (Rothery 1986), where the teacher and a group of children, or perhaps the whole class, produce a piece of writing together. This is a similar strategy to the 'wall story', where the teacher may scribe, but ideas from the group are included, modified, discussed or expanded by the children or by the teacher. This allows for discussion about language and about how the text is constructed within the context of language use.

☐ Read aloud from a variety of texts, not only narrative. This provides models of writing for a range of purposes.

☐ Provide access to a range of good quality models of the written product, especially to develop awareness of the range of styles and genres.

☐ Make use of conferences to work with children on the text itself. Focus on helping children to express meaning, rather than focusing narrowly on large numbers of surface errors. Some children may not have enough awareness of language as a system to respond to very open-ended conference questions, such as

How can I help you?' They may not be able to recognise how or where they need help. Be prepared to take on a heavier editing role with some children and to provide language when it is needed. This does not mean taking control of a child's writing — rather that guidance may need to be more explicit and directed. (*Can you remember how we said that when we were writing together?* rather than *Can you make this part more interesting?*)

☐ Encourage children to be independent writers by providing easy access to some of the tools for writing, such as models of text types, dictionaries, word banks (including high frequency words), checklists for proof reading and ideas for the steps in the writing process.

☐ Set topics for writing as well as allowing free choice. Provide models (for example, by innovating on text) when topics are given.

☐ Set writing tasks for pairs and groups as well as individuals. This is an opportunity for less confident and competent children to work collaboratively with children who will provide good models. The dictogloss technique described in the next section is an excellent strategy for group work.

☐ Use games and focused activities in developing specific language areas, such as those described on pp. 36-41 and 103. Cloze activities are particularly useful because they focus on a grammatical item or word within whole and connected text: the word(s) deleted can relate to the particular language item which you wish to focus on. To focus on the structure of particular text types, cut two short texts into sentences or paragraphs and have the children sort and order them. The two texts may be of the same genre (such as two reports — for example, one on *Bees* and one on *Cicadas*) or from two different genres, such as a narrative and a report.

☐ Allow children to write in their first language, or use written conversations (p. 56) with children in the early stages of literacy in English.

Using dictogloss

This is a technique developed by Ruth Wajnryb (1990). It has been adapted here to make it more suitable for younger learners. It is a particularly valuable teaching strategy because it involves and integrates the four skills of listening, speaking, reading and writing. It is also a way of using all these skills in a content area in which you wish to develop a knowledge base, such as science or social studies.

To begin with, the teacher reads a passage several times at normal speed. The passage can be related to any curriculum area. On first hearing the children listen without writing anything down, but during subsequent readings (once or twice more) they each write down as much as possible, particularly key words and phrases.

In pairs, the children discuss their notes and try to make them as complete as possible, adapting or expanding them if necessary. Each pair then joins with another pair to form a group of four, and again they pool their information. By using everyone's contribution the group should obtain a fairly accurate record of the original text.

Finally the group reconstructs the text in writing. They should aim at producing a coherent text which contains the same information as the original. It need not be identical to the original, but it is likely to be very similar. (Do not suggest that the groups should aim to 'use their own words', as part of the value in this exercise is that the children have an opportunity to use the language modelled by the text.)

An optional further stage is to display and talk about the groups' texts, although this is not essential to the process.

The value of dictogloss is that:

- it involves all four major skills

- it is a useful way of presenting new factual information across the curriculum

- it encourages children to listen for key points.

- it gives less competent children support, since they are not left to work alone

- it engages children in talk about content *and* talk about language

- it encourages children to work collaboratively, and in particular to listen to other people's ideas

- it provides the models of language which will be required at the writing stage.

A last word

Children learn to write by writing, but all children need support while they are doing so — after all, in learning to speak, they receive a great deal of quite specific help. In addition, children learning to write in a second language may not have the advantage of fluency in the spoken language. Children who are already disadvantaged in this way do not have unlimited time in which to learn to read and write; we should not assume that they will 'get there in the end'. This chapter has suggested some ways to plan intervention in the writing process, and to make it relevant to the development of each child.

CHAPTER TEN

A Whole School Response

A whole school focus

No one teacher can answer all the language needs of bilingual children alone. There is no such thing as a magic language 'fix' which will suddenly turn a child into a fluent English speaker. The language development of bilingual children needs to be seen as a whole school responsibility, and a school's response to their learning needs should be reflected in its policies and planning. In addition, classroom teachers who are aware of the issues related to learning in a second language will be better able to make the best use of the specialist skills of the ESL teacher in cooperative planning.

A role for the ESL teacher

ESL teachers can be involved in a variety of ways within the school. However they work, the aim should be to link their planning and teaching to the regular class program. Their role may include all or any of the following:

- teaching newly arrived children and children who are identified as needing additional support in English

- team-teaching with class teachers at year levels where there is an identified need for extra language support

- cooperatively planning with class teachers and ensuring that the class program takes into account children's language needs and the language demands of the curriculum

- designing or suggesting additional communicative language activities related to the classroom program
- alerting class teachers to resources available to support the language development of bilingual children
- assisting in the assessment and analysis of children's spoken and written language and informing class teachers about their language needs.

In schools where there are large numbers of second language learners, it is usually necessary to identify priority areas within the school. These priorities should reflect the needs of the children, not attempts to give each teacher an equal share of the ESL teacher's time, and decisions need to involve all teachers and the executive as well as the ESL teacher. As an example, this is how one ESL teacher works in a school with two classes at each grade level.

Four children in the school who are newly arrived receive face-to-face teaching on a daily basis. Depending on individual needs, this is either in-class or in a small group withdrawn from the classroom.

Ten children at various grade levels throughout the school have been identified as needing extra language support. (Four of them arrived during the last year.) They too receive regular face-to-face teaching, usually within their own class.

A large number of kindergarten children had little or no English on entry to school. The ESL teacher spends at least an hour of continuous time team-teaching in the classroom every day.

Years 1, 4 and 6 have been identified as having numbers of children in need of more language support. A decision was made to give more time to Year 1, with the expectation that early intervention would prevent later difficulties and consequently low student self-esteem.

A block of time is spent three times a week in Year 6.

The ESL teacher does not teach in a face-to-face role in other grade levels. She is involved in cooperatively planning with the grade level teachers, and language objectives are evident in all areas of their programs..

It is expected that these priorities may change during the year, and the program is to be evaluated at the end of the second term.

Including the community

Most of this book has been about language, and in particular the issues relating to teaching and learning in a second language. But educational outcomes for bilingual children, as for other children, are not only dependent on language. Jim Cummins

(1988) has identified the following four characteristics of schools which are supportive of minority language groups.

1 Language learning is promoted in all areas of the curriculum, within an interactive rather than teacher-centred classroom.

2 The language and culture of all students is incorporated in the school.

3 Teachers and other professionals within the school are advocates for second language learners in that they focus on the provision of appropriate classroom experiences, rather than seeing the students themselves as the source of perceived problems.

4 Minority community and parent participation is actively encouraged.

The ideas and suggestions put forward in earlier chapters have been posited upon the first three of these principles, and it is beyond the scope of this book to deal at length with issues raised by minority parent participation. However, there is no doubt about the strong link between successful learning outcomes and the degree to which parents are involved in the education process. Schools where there is genuine and active participation by parents have seen improved learning, and where schools have involved minority parents as partners and decision makers in their children's education, the parents have appeared to develop an increased sense of their worth that communicates itself to their children. (See, for example, the description of the 'Haringey Project' in Tizard, Schofield and Hewison 1982.)

The assumption is sometimes made that because particular parents are never seen at school, they are not interested in their children's schooling. This is rarely true. The great majority of parents want what is best for their children, are interested in their future and concerned about their education. There may be a number of reasons why some parents, particularly those from a minority ethnic background, do not willingly come into the school. For instance, it may be because of very different notions regarding the respective roles of teachers and parents. Our beliefs about parents and teachers as partners, however valid, are also cultural. They do not necessarily represent the notions of schooling, or of the role of teachers and schools, that are held by other cultural or ethnic groups. However, simply to explain away this issue as a cultural difference does not address the real needs of minority groups of children at school.

A parent program designed to include minority background parents must recognise cultural and linguistic difference in the same way as we recognise children's individual differences and starting points in planning appropriate language programs. But, like any good educational program, it must also aim at equality of opportunity. This means putting into place structures which will allow opportunities for parent involvement and participation to be *taken* as well as *offered*. There is often a lack of representation of many minority ethnic and lower socioeconomic groups within the official parent bodies of schools, with the result that they fail to represent the needs and concerns of parents who are unfamiliar with the culture of Australian schooling, and who may in addition have limited

English language skills. Such lack of representation is of course generally evident at many other levels of education and in many of the institutions of our society.

Involving parents within a school needs the cooperation and commitment of teachers to be successful, and the process is often a very long one. A great deal has been written about parental involvement in general, and so the following sections focus on issues relating to parents from minority linguistic and cultural backgrounds.

Communicating information

Effective communication with parents and local communities has been regular primary school practice for a long time. But communication is not always easy when parents speak little English and their language is not shared by anyone in the school. Many schools now regularly translate school notes, including newsletters and standard permission notes, into the major languages of the school community. Similarly they provide translations of information about admissions. Notes should be sent home bilingually (i.e both in the first language and in English) to avoid decisions about which language is appropriate for certain parents. Sometimes parents may be illiterate in their mother tongue as well as English, but this should not mean that no effort is made to translate notes. There will always be many members of the ethnic community who are literate, and, as Chapter 6 pointed out, a note to parents in the mother tongue is a visible sign of inclusion within the school. Notices around the school in the community languages indicating where the office and other buildings are, and welcome signs to visitors, are also symbols of inclusion.

Communication can also be a difficulty during parent-teacher interviews. Avoid using — or take care to explain — educational jargon or acronyms which are very familiar to teachers (such as *ESL, Special Ed., conferencing, first draft*) but may exclude others. If possible, provide interpreters in the major languages. Although parents may appear to be fairly fluent in day-to-day conversation, they may not have adequate English for discussing educational issues, and if this is the case, both parents and teachers will be disadvantaged. Not only may parents not understand what is being communicated to them, but they will not be actively involved. They may find it difficult to clarify key issues, ask questions or share their own knowledge of their child, and so teachers also miss out on important information.

If you use an interpreter, remember that you are still speaking to the parents. Maintain eye contact with them, not with the interpreter. A skilled interpreter should simply repeat what has been said by either party, and should not include his or her own opinions or asides. (A child should not be expected to interpret, since this may put all three people into difficult or embarrassing situations.)

To be partners in the educational process, parents need be informed about current teaching approaches. Differences in teaching methodology between their own school experiences and current practices often lead to confusion and misinterpretation. Sessions for parents which inform them of current curriculum are often most successful (and less language dependent) if they are 'hands-on' and involve parents carrying out some of the activities — for example, in maths or language —

that their children would take part in. When talk is involved in the activity, encourage parents to use the language they feel most comfortable with. You may have several groups, each using different languages, but, as with children, the notion of language choice is important, and many parents prefer to use English. Parent sessions should include time for discussion and questions. Again it is likely that this will be more successful if it includes opportunities for small group discussion, where parents less confident in English have the support of others from the same language background.

Whenever there is opportunity, offer practical suggestions to parents about how they can help their children at home. Some might feel that they are unable to help because of their own lack of English. Talk to parents about the value of the mother tongue and its importance in supporting their child's development of English. Stress the value of family talk and discussion in the mother tongue, including talk about what is happening at school. It may be helpful to show parents, especially parents of younger children, how you use the illustrations of a book for discussion (*What can you see? What do you think he might be doing? What do you think is going to happen next?*) and to point out that talk about books can occur in any language. If possible, use a bilingual parent or teacher to model this.

Involving parents

Most schools make a very great effort to make parents feel welcome. Informal gatherings such as morning teas, lunches or picnics offer opportunities for parents to meet in a non-threatening atmosphere. A multicultural school population has the potential to make such occasions a time when cultural diversity can be celebrated and shared! Just as important are informal contacts between parents and teachers. A welcoming school environment, like a supportive classroom, is a prerequisite for participation.

Parent networks can facilitate the process. Once rapport has been established with one or two parents from within an ethnic group, these parents can take a major role in the involvement of others through personal contact. They may be able to assist with verbal or written invitations to social events at school, and with explanations about camps and excursions.

Parents as helpers

Parents or other community volunteers are not substitutes for qualified teachers, and we should avoid excessive demands on willing parents which could result in the exploitation of an unpaid educational resource. However, many parents are willing to offer their skills, particularly their language skills, for specific purposes or perhaps for a limited period of time.

Parents who speak another language are a very valuable resource within the classroom. They can teach games and rhymes to children; help with cookery and craft; tell or record stories; help children writing in the mother tongue; teach songs and dances, and translate signs and notices. In addition, parents may be able

Parents working in the classroom help the teacher to individualise children's learning.

to help with more direct teaching, such as working with individual children in maths and language activities, helping children to produce bilingual books, and offering mother tongue support during regular classroom activities.

It is always important to provide some guidance for a parent helper. This may take the form of training sessions, or perhaps it can be provided through preparatory sessions during which the volunteer works alongside the teacher and sees how particular materials and strategies are used. Further suggestions about working with a parent helper and the kinds of activities in which they might be involved are to be found in Chapter 6.

Parents have a right to understand and be involved in the formal educational processes of their children and to share in related decision making. The way that individual schools respond to the linguistic and cultural diversity of their communities will determine to a large degree how far the participation of minority groups becomes a reality.

A framework for a whole school response

To help evaluate the kinds of support given to bilingual learners, this penultimate section contains examples of possible indicators of a school's responses to cultural and linguistic diversity. They are by no means definitive and every school would be able to add indicators of its own. It is presented as a framework based on the four key principles affecting students' learning which were listed earlier in this chapter. Although these principles are particularly relevant to the needs of bilingual learners, they are important to the learning of all children.

Language learning is promoted in all areas of the curriculum, within an interactive rather than teacher-centred classroom.

- Classroom programs indicate that there is a focus on language use and language development in all areas of the curriculum.

- Classroom programs relate to identified student language needs.

- Classroom programs indicate that there is a focus on developing higher level cognitive skills and critical thinking, rather than on simple recall.

- The classroom environment provides good models of oral and written English used for a variety of purposes.

- Children are regularly involved in collaborative learning through group and pair work.

- Teachers regularly interact with children on an individual basis.

- Children are actively encouraged to be independent learners by having access to information sources such as wordbanks, dictionaries, thesauruses, learning centres, computers and the library.

- Children are taught how to access information from these sources.

- There are classroom routines which encourage self-directed learning rather than teacher dependence (for example, contract systems and learning centres).

The language and culture of all students is incorporated in the school.

- There is evidence around the school and in the routines of school life that the children are from a variety of language backgrounds (for example, multilingual signs, school notices and newsletters, greetings, classsroom print, children's writing and mother tongue books).

- Bilingual learners feel free to use their mother tongue as a tool for learning, or are encouraged to do so (for example, by being grouped for this purpose at certain times, or through mother tongue support in the classroom).

- Resources are appropriate to children's experiences and are free of cultural stereotype and bias (for example, books in languages other than English, books in which children can identify themselves, tapes of stories in the mother tongue). Note that bias can also appear in what is omitted from the curriculum.

Information on this noticeboard is changed every week to reflect one of the school's twenty-nine ethnic groups.

- The curriculum includes the life experiences, culture and language of all children.
- Social or historical issues are presented from a standpoint that is not exclusively Anglo-Saxon (for example, the early white settlers of Australia can be presented as only the first among many who migrated subsequently).

- Some members of staff are from the cultural and linguistic backgrounds represented in the school, and it is the policy of the school to seek to employ such people (where possible within the employment structures of particular education systems).

Teachers and other professionals within the school are advocates for second language learners in that they focus on the provision of appropriate classroom experiences, rather than seeing the students themselves as the source of perceived problems.

- There is evidence that teachers have high expectations of all children.

- Children's language learning needs are assessed and classroom programs are designed to meet these needs.

- Assessment procedures are congruent with teaching practices, and possible cultural and linguistic bias in normed and standardised testing procedures is recognised.

- The self-esteem of children appears high.

- Grouping of children is flexible; it is not based on a deficit model where less competent children always work together, or where large groups of such children are regularly withdrawn from the class.

- The staff as a whole share understandings about language and literacy development, and have opportunities for exploring the teaching and learning issues implicit in second language development.

- Classroom programs are cooperatively planned with ESL teachers.

- In schools of high migrant density, some members of staff (other than specialist teachers) have training qualifications in ESL and Multicultural Education, and it is the policy of the school to seek to employ such people (where possible within the employment structure of particular education systems).

Minority community and parent participation is actively encouraged.

- Most parents from minority language backgrounds appear comfortable in entering the school and approaching teachers.

- Parents from minority language backgrounds are involved in school activities (for example, in the tuckshop or on excursions).

- Parents from minority language backgrounds are meaningfully involved in classroom activities and children's learning.

- Reporting procedures are in place which take the needs of minority language background parents into account (for example, by the use of interpreters in parent-teacher interviews).

• Information about the school and classroom practices is offered in the languages of the parents.

And a final note ...

All children have the right to leave school with the skills which will put them in control of their own lives. Their life choices will very largely depend on the skills, attitudes and values they have acquired at school. The skills they need are not simply the narrow ones of basic functional literacy, which, though necessary, are not sufficient for children who will be entering the work force in the twenty-first century. To participate in society, the children who are now in schools will need the skills to handle change. They will need to be able to access and make use of increasingly large amounts of information, to form and evaluate and challenge new ideas, and to think critically and creatively about their society and their environment.

Fundamental to all this is the ability to learn through language, and to understand and use it effectively. Many bilingual children will not reach their potential without planned intervention in their English language development. Those who have not developed to a high degree the language of the mainstream society will have much diminished power to participate in it, and will be likely to have their lives and life choices continually controlled by others.

In Australia most positions of power in the upper levels of education and other key areas, such as law and government, are still dominated by those from English speaking backgrounds. As in most other countries, our education systems tend to favour children who began school already familiar with the language of the classroom. If educators aim to provide equality of opportunity for all children, then we must also ensure that these opportunities can be taken. For children who are not competent in the language of the classroom, that means providing school experiences which acknowledge their different starting points and are designed to develop the language in which they are expected to learn.

Teachers know better than most that material resources are inadequate for the challenges they face daily in their classrooms. But individual teachers continue to have a great deal of power within their own classrooms, and so they will always be a major influence in how effectively children develop language.

The final thought in this book comes from Wittgenstein. It has relevance for everyone who is concerned with the language education of children, but particularly for those concerned with children who are learning to learn in their second language.

The limits of my language are the limits of my life.

Bibliography

Aird, E. and D. Lippmann. 1983. *English Is Their Right*. Melbourne: AE Press.

Anderson, J. 1982. "The concept of cohesion and its importance to teachers of reading." *Reading Around* 10(2).

Anderson, R. and P. Pearson. 1984. "A schema-theoretic view of basic processes in reading comprehension." *Handbook of Reading*. Ed. P. Pearson. London: Longman.

Anstey, M. and G. Bull. 1989. "From teaching to learning: translating monitoring into planning and practice." *Monitoring Children's Language Development*. Ed. E. Daly. Portsmouth, NH: Heinemann.

Cambourne, B. and J. Turbill. 1987. *Coping with Chaos*. Portsmouth, NH: Heinemann.

Cardenas, A. 1986. "The role of native language instruction in bilingual education." *Phi Delta Kappan* (January).

Carrell, P. and J. Eisterhold. 1983. "Schema theory and ESL reading pedagogy." *TESOL Quarterly* 17(4).

Chapman, L.J. 1983. *Reading Development and Cohesion*. London: Heinemann.

Christie, F. 1990. *Literacy for a Changing World*. Melbourne: ACER.

Clayton, L. 1984. *When Do You Bow in Australia?* Sydney: AFS International Exchanges.

Corson, D. 1988. *Oral Language across the Curriculum*. New York: Taylor & Francis.

Cummins, J. 1988. "From multicultural to anti-racist education." *Minority Education: From Shame to Struggle*. Eds. T. Skutnabb-Kangas and J. Cummins. New York: Taylor & Francis.

Cummins, J. and M. Swain. 1986. *Bilingualism in Education*. London: Longman.

Derewianka, B. 1990. *Exploring How Texts Work*. Portsmouth, NH: Heinemann.

Dufficy, P. 1989. "Integrating a student with minimal or no English in a mainstream primary classroom." *Topics in ESL* 8. Sydney: NSW Department of Education Multicultural Education Centre.

Dwyer, J., ed. 1989. *A Sea of Talk*. Portsmouth, NH: Heinemann.

Foster, D. 1989. "Incorporating teachers' aides into the classroom." *Topics is ESL* 8. Sydney: NSW Department of Education Multicultural Education Centre.

Goodman, K. 1967. "Reading: a psycholinguistic guessing game." *Journal of the Reading Specialist* 6(1).

Gorman, T. 1985. "Language assessment and language teaching: innovation and interaction." *Language and Learning: An Interactional Perspective.* Eds. G. Wells and J. Nicholls. New York: Taylor & Francis.

Halliday, M.A. 1989. *Spoken and Written Language.* New York: Oxford University Press.

Halliday, M.A. and R. Hasan. 1976. *Cohesion in English.* New York: Longman.

Holdaway, D. 1979. *The Foundations of Literacy.* Portsmouth, NH: Heinemann.

Holdaway, D. 1991. *Independence in Reading; A Handbook on Individualized Procedures, Third Edition.* Portsmouth, NH: Heinemann.

Hornsby, D., D. Sukarna, and J. Parry, eds. 1988. *Read On: A Conference Approach to Reading.* Portsmouth, NH: Heinemann.

Houlton, D. 1985. *All Our Languages: A Handbook for the Multilingual Classroom.* London: Edward Arnold.

Johnson, T. and D. Louis. 1987. *Literacy Through Literature.* Portsmouth, NH: Heinemann.

Lambert, W.E. and E. Peal. 1962. "The relation of bilingualism to intelligence." *Psychological Monographs* 76.

Levin, A. 1981. *Has It Ever Occurred to You?* Sydney: Sydney College of Education Multicultural Centre.

Levine, J. 1990. *Bilingual Learners and the Mainstream Curriculum.* New York: Taylor & Francis.

Lock, S. 1983. *Second-language Learners in the Classroom.* Canberra: Materials Production Curriculum Branch.

Mansfield, J. and S. Pledge. 1983. *No English.* Melbourne: Child Migrant Services, Education Department of Victoria.

Phillips, J. 1987. "How similar is learning a second language to learning a first?" *Early Language Development of Bilingual Children.* Ed. A. Hodge. Sydney: Sydney College of Advanced Education Multicultural Centre.

Rothery, J. 1986. "Teaching writing in the primary school: a genre-based approach to the development of writing abilities." *Working Papers in Linguistics* 4. Sydney: University of Sydney.

Saville-Troike, M. 1976. *Foundations for Teaching English as a Second Language.* Old Tappan, N.J.: Prentice Hall.

Skutnabb-Kangas, T. 1984. *Bilingualism or Not: The Education of Minorities.* New York: Taylor & Francis.

Skutnabb-Kangas, T. and J. Cummins., eds. 1988. *Minority Education: Fram Shame to Struggle.* New York: Taylor & Francis.

Skutnabb-Kangas, T. and T. Toukamaa. 1976. *Teaching Migrant Children's Mother Tongue and Learning the Language of the Host Community.* Helsinki: Finnish National Commission for UNESCO.

Smith, F. 1978. *Reading.* Cambridge: Cambridge University Press.

Spolsky, B., ed. 1972. *The Language Education of Bilingual Children.* Rowley, MA: Newbury House.

Tizard, J., W. Scofield, and J. Hewison. 1982. "Collaboration between teachers and parents in assisting children's reading." *British Journal of Educational Psychology* 52.

Vygotsky, L.S. 1962. *Thought and Language*. Cambridge, MA: MIT Press.

Wajnryb, R. 1990. *Grammar Dictation*. Oxford: Oxford University Press.

Wells, G. 1981. *Learning through Interaction*. Cambridge: Cambridge University Press.

Wells, G. and J. Nicholls, eds. 1985. *Language and Learning: An Interactional Perspective*. New York: Taylor & Francis.

Wiles, S. 1985. "Language learning in multi-ethnic classrooms: strategies for supporting bilingual students." *Language and Learning: An Interactional Perspective*. G. Wells and J. Nicholls, eds. New York: Taylor & Francis.

Wong-Filmore, L. 1982. "Instructional language as linguistic input: second language learning in classrooms." *Communicating in the Classroom*. L. Wilkinson, ed. New York: Academic.